DISRUPT
EVERYTHING

DISRUPT
EVERYTHING
AND WIN

TAKE CONTROL OF YOUR FUTURE

James Patterson
Patrick Leddin, PhD

C

CENTURY

CENTURY

UK | USA | Canada | Ireland | Australia
India | New Zealand | South Africa

Century is part of the Penguin Random House group of companies
whose addresses can be found at global.penguinrandomhouse.com

Penguin Random House UK,
One Embassy Gardens, 8 Viaduct Gardens, London SW11 7BW

penguin.co.uk
global.penguinrandomhouse.com

Penguin
Random House
UK

First published 2025
001

Printed and bound in Great Britain by Clays Ltd, Elcograf S.p.A.

The authorised representative in the EEA is Penguin Random House Ireland,
Morrison Chambers, 32 Nassau Street, Dublin D02 YH68

A CIP catalogue record for this book is available from the British Library

ISBN: 978–1–529–96267–3 (hardback)
ISBN: 978–1–529–96268–0 (trade paperback)

MIX
Paper | Supporting
responsible forestry
FSC
www.fsc.org   FSC® C018179

Penguin Random House is committed to a sustainable future
for our business, our readers and our planet. This book is made
from Forest Stewardship Council® certified paper.

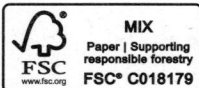

CONTENTS

CONTENTS

CONTENTS

CONTENTS

DISRUPT
EVERYTHING

Preface

Here's a promise: *Disrupt Everything* will help you deal with the most powerful and misunderstood force in this fast-changing world — disruption.

Disruption is a force of change.

Some of us, maybe most of us, stubbornly resist change, even when it's clearly in our best interests. But resisting change can leave us left out, left behind, and left feeling lost, cheated, and angry.

It shouldn't be that way. And if we're open to effecting change, it doesn't have to be that way.

It's like turning the page in a new book. Like this one.

Inside this book is a story — the reader's story. It will have a beginning, a middle, and an end. It will contain some drama. The story will have a powerful, engaging beginning, signifying a commitment to a certain path in life. It will have a compelling middle, with some surprises and some adjustments. And it should have a satisfying ending, leaving you with the knowledge that you're prepared for future disruptions.

And there *will* be future disruptions.

In 2022, I visited Nashville several times while Dolly Parton and I were cowriting a novel, *Run, Rose, Run*. That February, I visited my old graduate school, Vanderbilt University, to give a guest lecture titled "The Power of Disruptions" to business students in Professor Patrick Leddin's leadership class.

I began by challenging (disrupting) the students in an unusual way. I asked them if they were living a good life. Or had they been getting on one treadmill after another for most of their lives? Was that treadmill routine satisfying for them? Basically, were they happy?

I told the students how several significant disruptions had led to my becoming CEO of the country's leading advertising agency, J. Walter Thompson. And how I had then disrupted my life in a major way by changing careers and eventually becoming the bestselling writer in the world.

Finally, I confessed to them that, because of disruptions, I'd been in love with two wonderful women—and had married one of them. I reassured the students that I wanted all of them to lead good, satisfying lives and that managing disruptions would be important—more important than they could imagine.

This book came about because of that disruptive lecture.

Today, whenever I give a speech—whether to a corporate group, to college students, or to people at a book event—I ask the audience members whether they are living good lives. And now I'll ask you the same question: Are you living a good life? Are you passionate about your job? About your employer? About your future? How is your family life? How are your relationships with friends and coworkers? Are you able to balance your work life with your personal life?

I love my job. That's because I don't work for a living; I play for a living. The reason for this—100 percent—has to do with managing disruption.

Equally important, or maybe even more important, has been the effect of disruptions on my home life. I love my wife. I sometimes joke that if Sue ever leaves me, I'm going with her. I love our son, Jack. The three of us have always discussed and negotiated significant changes—disruptions—in our lives.

Disruption can be scary, but it can also be an agent for positive change. Virtually every company, and virtually every employee from top to bottom, needs to be open to disruption and play a part in positive change. That's right: Everybody has a part to play.

My successes, as well as my weathering of bad luck and personal tragedy, have arisen from my ability to understand and make use of disruption in positive ways.

I became the CEO of J. Walter Thompson North America at thirty-six. I got there by disrupting the norm, which spurred growth and much higher profits for the firm.

When I was twenty-four, I was living out of a tiny room in a low-rent hotel on West 51st Street in New York City. The wallpaper in the room had thousands of pentagons on it, and some former occupant had drawn an X through every single pentagon. I needed to get out of there, fast.

But how? Back then, I didn't know I needed a disruption, but I did need one. Badly.

To secure an entry-level job as an advertising copywriter, you were required to present a portfolio of clever ads. I wanted to work at J. Walter Thompson because Thompson was the biggest and most powerful ad agency, but I had never taken an advertising or marketing course.

What I did was disrupt the hiring process. I hand-delivered a portfolio of ads to Thompson's New York office. This wasn't a disruption; it was the status quo. But the next week, I delivered a second portfolio. And the third week, I delivered a third portfolio. I was definitely disrupting the normal process at JWT.

The company hired me in the fourth week.

Years later, when I was promoted to head of the New York office at JWT, the product wasn't good. We needed better personnel. It was time for another disruption. We ran an ad in the *New York Times*. The headline was straightforward: "Write If You Want Work." There were six questions, six problems to solve. I promised to hire writers based on the test and a single interview.

Here is one of the problems applicants had to solve: "The ingredients listed on the tin of baked beans reads: 'Beans, Water, Tomatoes, Sugar, Salt, Modified Starch, Vinegar, Spices. Make it sound mouthwatering.'"

Over the course of the following years, we hired over forty writers based on that single very disruptive ad.

During this time at Thompson, I was writing novels on the side. Writing was my real passion, my dream job.

Next came the biggest disruption of my life. It happened on the New Jersey Turnpike, of all places. One beautiful summer Sunday, I had to leave my house and go back to work in New York City. As I headed north, traffic on the turnpike was bumper-to-bumper. But on the other side, the southbound side, there were almost no cars.

Every ten or fifteen seconds, I would hear this sound:

Whoosh.

Whoosh.

That was the sound of a car passing in the opposite direction, and that sound—*whoosh*—led me to the next disruption. A really big one. I realized that my mission was to get on the other side of the highway. My whole life was going in the wrong direction.

I didn't need to be in bumper-to-bumper traffic heading to a job I no longer really cared about. I needed to be on the other side of the road. I needed to be writing novels full-time. But to do that, I had to walk away from a powerful, high-paying job.

So I quit my steady job. It wasn't an easy decision.

My writing partner on *Disrupt Everything,* Patrick Leddin, also took a leap of faith when he left his prestigious role as a professor at Vanderbilt University to speak to audiences around the world about disruption.

These are examples of big disruptions—the kind you'll learn to make when they're needed.

Disrupt Everything will help you harness the power of small and big disruptions and teach you why sometimes, choosing *not* to disrupt is equally important.

When I started writing full-time, there was an unspoken rule in the publishing industry that most authors should only publish one book a year. That rule didn't make sense to me, so I started writing two, then three, then more than half a dozen books a year. At first, my publisher, Little, Brown, resisted — but then the people there saw that disruption working like nothing they had ever seen before.

Next I started collaborating with cowriters. Another big disruption. Then I took up cowriting with famous people and groups — President Bill Clinton, Dolly Parton, Viola Davis, the Albert Einstein estate, and the Michael Crichton estate. More successful disruptions followed.

Advertising books on television — a first for my publisher. Writing in many different genres — suspense, love stories, kids' books, graphic novels, narrative nonfiction, memoir. I created BookShots — novellas that can be read in around the time it takes to watch a movie.

As I write these pages, I'm the bestselling writer in the world.

At least that's what my publisher tells me.

Of course, the other side of the coin is that unfortunately, we all have to deal with disruptions in life that involve setbacks and personal tragedies — the kind of disruptions capable of sinking any of us without a trace.

In fact, as I write, our world has never felt more chaotic than right now.

But we can be better prepared. For economic disruptions like the ones in 2008 and 2020. For worldwide disruptions like COVID-19. Even for personal medical emergencies that can break our hearts.

When I was in my thirties, I was in love with a very special woman named Jane Hall Blanchard. Suddenly, out of nowhere, we found out that Jane had an inoperable brain tumor. But we never let the fact that she was dying control us. Jane lived each day as well and as bravely as she could. Through her illness, I learned to deal with death— that cruel, unforgiving, inevitable disrupter.

And you know what? Unpredictable disruptions are going to keep coming at us like speeding meteors. They always do.

The purpose of *Disrupt Everything* is to make disruption a positive force, helping you change your life for the better.

Our mission is to help ordinary people—people like you, like Patrick, and like me—deal effectively with unexpected disruptions. We want to help people lead better lives by managing—and even profiting from— disruption rather than letting disruption manage us.

Where do you want to go?

In business, and in life, there really isn't a ceiling. The best way to demonstrate that is to take some chances. Enthusiasm and hunger are trademarks of people who succeed. Those are familiar qualities, right?

What you're doing is not easy, but you've learned a lot of lessons along the way. Now is the time to start practicing them. And I mean really *practice*. When you practice, you perform a task repeatedly until you get better and better at it. Practice is another way of making change — disrupting your daily reality to produce a better result.

So how do you get there?

My own daily goal is to get back to doing what I want to do. Nowadays, that's less about being the number one novelist than it is about having a balanced life. If I were to create a blueprint, or a mission statement, it might look something like this:

There's a story for everybody.
Don't get in the way of the story.
Tap into something in the psyche.
Get interested in the people in the middle.
Provide cathartic emotional experiences.

Now you try it.

Say you're an employee moving up the ranks in the company where you work. Say you have a talent for logistics. Your mission statement might look something like this:

Streamline the process.
Figure out what's not working and why.
Figure out what is working — and amplify the
    company's strengths through your actions.

11

Or say there's a product that's been lighting up your imagination. You've created it and become an entrepreneur. You've founded a company and a brand to market that product.

At its simplest, a brand is just a symbol of the trust established between a group of people and what you're offering them—just trust. *If you pick up product X, you won't be able to stop using it.* That's it: Go ahead and make your company indispensable.

Make your product the one that stands out.
Take the mystery out of the business.
Reach more people—and different kinds of people—by listening to their feedback.

Here's a mission statement for us all, no matter what our professional roles are.

Get your business life in sync with your personal life.
Your loved ones want the best for you.
Give them *your* best.

The heart and mind can help you to get serious about a job, about changing careers, about starting a car wash, about following a leader's vision at work, about improving someone else's vision through your own ideas. It's the heart and mind working together that help you select a path moving forward and commit to it. That's definitely what happened to me as a writer. I also think it's what happened to Patrick when he saw an opportunity.

Large or small, all companies and institutions have mission statements. For these to be best put into practice, every employee needs to buy in — but these same employees also need to be willing to change how they do their jobs in small and large ways. *They need to be able to disrupt.* Employees who want to advance, at any level, have to be seen as positive disrupters.

Entrepreneurs — anyone who wants to start their own businesses — absolutely have to understand how to make disruption work positively for them.

Disrupt Everything recognizes and supports the essential connection between the business life and the personal life of everyone, using positive disruption to improve lives.

That's the bottom line: leading a better life.

So let's start. It's time for your first disruption. We'll make this easy, even fun, and it will help you live a better life.

—James Patterson

Part I
Fire, Fuel, and Four Facts

Chapter 1

The Fire Inside You

Identifying your intentions is a deeply personal endeavor. Activating them is a courageous one.

Megan Piphus can't believe the email that's just popped up in her inbox. It's from Matt Vogel, a producer for the Emmy Award–winning *Sesame Street,* one of the world's longest-running TV programs, and a principal *Sesame Street* Muppet performer. He's known for playing Big Bird, the Count, and, since 2017, the Disney Muppet Kermit the Frog. The friends and neighbors on Manhattan's fictional Sesame Street have entertained and educated millions of children over the course of more than fifty years.

Megan grew up in Cincinnati, Ohio, as one of those children. She celebrated her third birthday with a *Sesame Street*–themed party. Zoe was her favorite Muppet, though Megan was also later intrigued by Abby Cadabby.

Megan took piano lessons and dance lessons. Her father, a pastor, encouraged her to sing in the church choir. "In small circles, I had a hard time opening up and overcoming shyness," Megan says. "But onstage, I felt like I had strength."

Her appetite for performing was further ignited at ten years old, when she saw a female ventriloquist captivating an audience. "As soon as I realized that puppetry was an art form that you could learn," Megan says, "I wanted to be the person that was onstage or behind the curtain working the puppet and doing ventriloquism."

Megan's mom is an educator and a speech pathologist. When Megan told her about the new skill she wanted to learn, her mom called several local library branches to ask: "Do you have tapes on how to do ventriloquism?"

A vocal technique that dates back to ancient Greece, ventriloquism involves the illusion of a performer "throwing her voice," making sound seem to come from a different source, like a puppet. It often requires not only talking, but singing and acting.

Megan watched those videos "back and forth" and, using the puppet her mom bought for her, spent hours practicing her new techniques. She first put on shows for her family, then, eventually, for her classmates at school, where her teachers gave her praise and encouragement.

By sixth grade, she was entertaining the entire student body, and as a teenager, Megan was traveling the nation, performing at schools and churches. As her experience grew, so did her successes, leading to an appearance on *The Tonight Show.* Another appearance, on *America's Got Talent,* earned her Yes votes from all four judges.

"I don't think people realize just how hard that is," Howard Stern said of Megan's performance during that broadcast. "You have an incredible singing voice, [it] is remarkable that you can do it, not move your lips, operate these puppets, make them come to life."

"Stunning," added Howie Mandel. "You are amazingly talented. You have an amazing singing voice, a range from pop to opera, and I, just now, have become a fan of ventriloquism."

Fast-forward to the day Megan gets that email from Matt Vogel, the *Sesame Street* producer. During the show's COVID-19 pandemic hiatus, Matt and his team have been going through submissions and have come across Megan's long-ago audition package. *Are you still interested in joining the* Sesame Street *cast?*

Megan's heart races as she reads the words. *Is this real?* She's working full-time in real estate, but joining the *Sesame Street* cast has been a lifelong dream.

Despite the challenges of auditioning and training virtually during the pandemic while pregnant with her second child, Megan pounces on the opportunity.

"It was a hard balance having a full-time job in real estate and also starting a career at *Sesame Street*. I have a family and two young children," she says. "I just needed to take a leap of faith to move into the television industry and puppetry full-time."

All signs point to it being the right decision. "Within a couple of weeks of leaving my career in real estate, the news broke about me being the first Black woman puppeteer on *Sesame Street*."

Megan also makes history when she debuts Gabrielle, a Black Muppet vibrantly costumed in an orange cardigan, patterned skirt, hot-pink shoes, and matching hair ties in her Afro puffs. Gabrielle lives on Sesame Street, is six and three-quarters years old, and enjoys singing, dancing, and cooking. She even teaches her good friends Elmo and Abby Cadabby about racism.

"I realized in that moment that I had made history in a show that had already been around for over fifty years," says Megan. "We're able to tackle very heavy topics, and I know I'm just training and leading the next generation to be kinder and smarter and stronger. And I get to teach my own children through *Sesame Street*. I know I'm creating content that they're going to watch at home."

And she's excited about the ripple effects. "I realized that it would open doors for other Black women, women of color, little boys of color, entering the entertainment space to really see that they can be absolutely anything—no matter how niche or unique."

In 2023, Sesame Workshop partners with toy makers to release Gabrielle plushies, including one that talks and sings the Muppet's signature song, "I Love My Hair." Megan posts an unboxing video on Instagram, captioned "My first time hearing my voice on the Gabrielle doll 😣 😭."

Visibly moved, she hugs the doll with tears in her eyes and declares, "Oh man, I wish I had this as a little girl." Under her video she writes, "Go out and get the Gabrielle plush doll for your kids! This girl is making a difference. This is not an ad; I'm not getting anything from this beyond being a light for self-positivity and love."

Megan's achievements stem from igniting the **Fire Inside.**

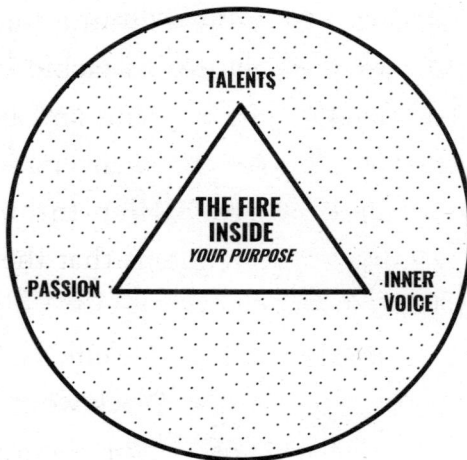

Just like Megan, you have a fire inside. It overlaps with your **Talent, Inner Voice,** and **Passion.**

Talent involves special ability—both what you're good at and also what you're truly *great* at.

Everyone has a distinct talent that sets them apart from the crowd. It could be an innate skill: creative flair, spatial relations, nurturing friends and family. It could be a learned expertise: strategic planning, entrepreneurship, auto repair, architectural design.

Everyone also has an inner voice, also known as a **Conscience.** The messages it broadcasts to your brain through feelings and instinct are informed by a powerful combination of experience, knowledge, and belief. Tuning in to your conscience motivates you to address the world's unmet needs in ways that inherently feel right to you.

Passion is the spark that lights the fire inside, igniting your enthusiasm and commitment.

Passion stirs up excitement that goes far beyond the prospect of making money. It's what drives you to dive into projects or activities you genuinely enjoy, the kind of stuff you'd happily do even if you weren't getting paid. There's so much value in finding your own voice. Doing work you are passionate about fulfills you with a priceless sense of personal satisfaction.

Megan possesses the ability to be a world-class entertainer (talent); she recognizes and responds to the world's need for joy and the teaching of valuable lessons (inner voice); and she experiences the exhilaration of doing something she loves (passion).

Build Your Fire on a Strong Foundation

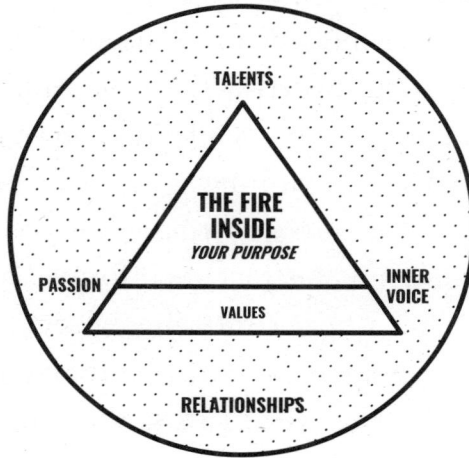

Whether out of fear, misunderstanding, or lack of motivation, far too many people aren't clear on who they are and what they want to be. Those who shy away from this deeply personal endeavor are left to draw on others' energy or thoughtlessly go with the flow established by those around them.

Discovering the fire inside is only the beginning. The harder part is living in alignment—especially in the face of life's many disruptions. Yet when handled wisely, disruptions can become fuel to ignite the fire. The fire inside burns with your **Purpose.**

It begins with the tough task of articulation. Identifying your intentions out loud or in writing is a deeply personal endeavor. Activating them is a courageous one.

Ask yourself: What does living with integrity mean to you? How do you demonstrate it in your daily actions? Here's the hard truth—living a life that doesn't align with your values smothers the fire inside you, quenching your ability to thrive and express your true self.

When your fire is built on a strong foundation, its heat grounds you during challenging times, and its flames can elevate you to heights beyond your expectations. The fire inside you burns brightest when it's built on values you've identified and defined and are willing to put into action. Honesty. Responsibility. Compassion. Respect. These are a few examples of the fundamental beliefs and principles that guide the decisions you make every hour of every day.

Keep reading, and you will learn how to burn that fuel.

Purpose Versus Mission

People often throw around the words *purpose* and *mission* interchangeably, but there's a distinction between them that's worth remembering.

Your *purpose* is your deepest, most core reason for

existence. What gives your life meaning? Why do you do what you do? Your purpose is broad and timeless, even when your job or other life circumstances change.

Your *mission* is a more concrete expression of how you are living out your purpose. It defines what you're trying to achieve, how you want to contribute to the world, and what priorities are guiding your actions, providing clear direction when you get out of bed each morning. And it may change over time as you accomplish certain goals and set new objectives.

"I want young children seeing themselves represented on television to be filled with confidence and to know they are special," Megan says. Her purpose is entertaining people—that will never change. But her mission evolves as her circumstances evolve, throughout her career and her personal life.

"On my vision board years ago, I pinned *Sesame Street*," Megan says. "And now I'm on the cast." She doesn't stop there, adding images of Emmy Awards to the vision board—and in 2021, wins two. "All of that manifestation has been a result of me dreaming and believing that I'm capable of the biggest dreams coming true."

Defining Disruption

Disrupt Everything. Those are powerful words.

The research behind them is substantial.

Because words *are* powerful, conversations form the basis of *Disrupt Everything*—detailed conversations with people who've chosen to make disruptions the basis for meaningful and lasting change in their lives.

Connecting with disrupters such as Megan led to comprehensive one-on-one interviews with hundreds of people, from household names to unsung heroes, each of whom has forged a distinctly disruptive professional or personal path.

Countless hours exploring how thousands of people follow their dreams led to the clear conclusion that the quest for the good life extends beyond individual pursuits.

Relationships aren't simply a means to an end; they are the richest part of the journey.

Defining Positive Disruption

One thing that consistently stands out as the greatest challenge, and greatest opportunity, when it comes to *"living a good life"* is a person's willingness to disrupt everything—and win. In other words, when you choose to be a **Positive Disrupter**, you become someone who fosters dynamic teams, transforms organizations, revitalizes industries, builds meaningful relationships, and breathes life and love into family.

Think about how Megan's fire inside created a better life not only for herself but also for millions of *Sesame Street* viewers. Becoming a positive disrupter can start a ripple effect in countless unpredictable directions.

Your definition of "winning" is as unique as you are. What does living a good life mean to you?

Think about that for a moment.

Does it mean you are eager to get out of bed every morning?

Does it mean you enjoy a stable income that lets you support the people you love?

Does it mean you're part of a team that's making a meaningful impact on the world?

Does it mean you have reached the life goals you dreamed of when you were younger?

Answering these questions means unlocking the secret of a powerful paradox: the very disruptions that threaten to derail you from the path to a good life are the same ones that can propel you closer to it. Getting clear on your fire inside is the essential first step toward creating that good life.

~~~~~~~~~~~~~~~~~~~~~~~~~~~~~~~~

Positive Disrupter Move

Claim the Day

Before your feet hit the floor, pause. One breath. One thought. *Why am I here today?* Move with purpose, not autopilot.

Still uncertain about your purpose and values? To reflect on your personal mission or that of your team, turn to "Part VII: Your Positive Disrupter Toolkit" and check out "Tool 1: Identify the Fire Inside You" and "Tool 2: Craft Your Mission Statement."

~~~~~~~~~~~~~~~~~~~~~~~~~~~~~~~~

Chapter 2
The Fuel for the Fire Inside

Every disruption, big or small, good or bad, has the potential to unleash something amazing.

"I've lost my job again."

As Bevin Farrand approaches her fortieth birthday, the job promotion she's been expecting turns out to be a layoff.

It's a stinging blow. What's worse, instability is becoming an unwelcome presence in her work life. Yet within this turmoil she sees a glimmer of opportunity—a chance to chart a new path. The former marketing brand director gets certified as a coach and within two months secures her first contract—to create a marketing strategy for a nonprofit organization.

"I'm going to start my own business," she tells her

husband, Mark, father of their young daughter and son.

Mark values stability. He earned his degree in mechanical engineering and works as a vehicle research engineer. Bevin's own professional uncertainty is generating what she jokingly describes as "convulsions in Mark's mind," even as she harbors doubts of her own about whether they should postpone her big birthday trip.

Is it really the right time to take the trip to France we've been planning to celebrate my fortieth?

Bevin and Mark decide to go for it, setting out for a romantic five-day trip sans kids to the Nouvelle-Aquitaine region, in the southwestern part of the country, and its famed port city, Bordeaux. They cross the bridge over the Garonne River, walk the cobblestone streets, and explore the wine-producing district of Médoc.

"I'm spending my fortieth birthday with the love of my life, reconnecting to who we were before we had kids, before we got married," Bevin tells Mark.

Mark, too, revels in the freedom that travel allows. In a testament to the strength of their reconnection, he says, "I feel like I'm rediscovering the real you."

Hour by hour, they strengthen their relationship. Day by day, their shared vision of the future becomes clearer, and together they make the momentous decision to pursue having a third child via in vitro fertilization, just like their first two.

They return home to an undetectable ticking time bomb.

Five days later, Mark passes away in his sleep. His cause of death: undiagnosed heart disease.

We had no idea this was coming. It's an unfathomable goodbye.

A grieving Bevin is overcome by loss. Yet she's determined to forge ahead, not only with her professional plans but also with the ones she and Mark made for their family.

She founds a movement and calls it Take the DAMN Chance. Its pillars are risk-taking, defining a vision, and creating newness in life. She advocates for people to go ahead and pursue their "crazy" dreams; and if they're too overwhelmed to start big, to instead start with "microactions," small steps that can kick-start goals and grow into significant results.

Despite the "emotional complexities and societal pressures" of welcoming a third child as a solo parent, Bevin says, "expanding our family, even in Mark's absence, feels like a testament to our love and the life we dreamed of together." Their third child, another daughter, is born twenty months after Mark's death, from an embryo the couple had previously frozen during their earlier rounds of IVF. "There was never a doubt in my mind that I wanted to bring another piece of Mark into the world. Making it happen took work, but having her was the easiest decision I've ever made," says Bevin.

Bevin is a positive disrupter. By surviving the loss of Mark and fueling the fire inside her, she stands as a beacon of hope, encouraging all who have gone through deeply challenging experiences to embrace life's unpredictability, face their fears, and seize every opportunity.

The Tough Reality of Life's Disruptions

Imagine if wanting something was enough to make it happen. Life would be a breeze, but it would lose much of its depth and satisfaction. The real essence of living a good life lies in the grit and hard work it takes to realize your aspirations. Your journey is fraught with disruptions and challenges, requiring you to be disciplined, set goals, and work effectively with others. Merely acquiring and perfecting skills without a sense of where you are going may just allow you to move more quickly and efficiently down the wrong path in life.

To set the stage for this exploration, let's first examine four fundamental facts that are at play in both your personal and professional lives.

Fact 1: The Status Quo Is a Deceptive Little Devil

Familiarity and predictability masquerade as a safe haven, giving a false sense of security and contentment. This deceptive comfort zone can stifle growth and prevent you from pursuing the extraordinary. It can also mislead you into thinking that what is good today is guaranteed to remain just as good in the future.

Fact 2: You're Wired to Disrupt

Within you lies a dormant capacity for innovation and change. This inherent ability is like a sleeping giant, ready to awaken and reshape the world around you. It's up to you to hear the call and seize the opportunity.

Fact 3: Relationships Provide Headwinds and Tailwinds

Relationships have the profound power to either ignite and nourish your inner fire or dampen and extinguish your zest and creativity. The connections you cultivate can lift you up, pushing you toward your dreams, or they can pull you down, anchoring you in place. You can also do the same for others. Recognizing the significant role relationships play in fanning the flames of your inner disrupter, or smothering it under the weight of negativity and small-mindedness, is essential.

Fact 4: Your Time Here Is Finite—Make It Count in Ways That Matter

The singular life journey you embark upon is precious and finite. Recognizing its brevity should compel you to seize every moment and push you to live with purpose and passion.

You have only one life to live.

You have only one opportunity to invest in a relationship or cherish a moment.

You have only one chance to be on the team you are on or build the organization you are building.

You have only today to make a difference in the lives of others.

Make it count.

In the following chapters, unpack these four fundamental facts in the quest to fuel your fire inside.

But first, let's get back to the initial question. Be honest with yourself. Are you living a good life?

If your response is not a resounding yes, this book might spark you to make a significant pivot, because it will encourage you to realize that the power to alter your situation lies in your hands and that all it takes to start the process is a shift in your perspective. But be prepared: Achieving a good life isn't always straight-forward. It might mean letting go of material posses-sions, job titles, or relationships you once cherished but that now hold you back. Or it could require a dras-tic shift in your life's direction. These decisions are tricky. If they were easy, you would have already made them.

Suppose your response to the good-life question is a resounding yes. Well done! But a word of caution: The status quo is a deceptive little devil, and your habits today might be inadequate to confront what lies ahead. Remember that today's contentment isn't guaranteed to be there tomorrow — expectations change, relation-ships evolve (and devolve), health scares emerge, fam-ily dynamics shift, and work expectations fluctuate.

Living a good life often involves bold choices, such as changing careers, ending a chapter, reimagining your journey, sacrificing immediate pleasures for long-term rewards, or exploring capabilities you didn't know you had. In a work context, it can involve challenging your team to tackle bold new projects, new strategies, or new markets. But it also involves the small — nearly imperceptible — daily steps that move you in the right direction over time.

Regardless of how you answered the good-life ques-tion, here's the reality: Change is a constant companion.

Positive Disrupter Move

Say "I'm Done"

End it. Not because you quit, but because you are done making space for what doesn't fit in your life.

Chapter 3

Fact 1: The Status Quo Is a Deceptive Little Devil

It takes bravery and courage to rebuild a life one small task at a time.

Scottish mountaineer Jamie Andrew and his climbing partner, Jamie Fisher, are both seasoned sportsmen up for any challenge.

During a January skiing holiday, they find themselves near Les Droites — a formidable four-thousand-meter peak in the Mont Blanc massif, in the French Alps — and decide to scale its north face, a one-thousand-meter vertical climb.

They set off, monitoring a gigantic low-pressure system over the Atlantic. Midway through their ascent, the air pressure in the atmosphere shifts, sweeping the system across Europe and unleashing a catastrophic snowstorm over the Alps.

They summit, but there, at the most vulnerable point on the mountain, the weather turns fully against them. They have no other option but to hunker down in their sleeping bags and endure the onslaught on a tiny, icy ledge.

For five grueling days and nights they exist in a frozen hell. While they await the rescue team, winds whip up to ninety miles per hour. Temperatures plunge to minus twenty-two degrees Fahrenheit, afflicting both climbers with hypothermia.

By the time help finally arrives on the sixth morning, Jamie Andrew is barely clinging to consciousness. Jamie Fisher's case proves fatal. As Jamie Andrew is airlifted to a hospital for treatment, he's able to register the haunting image of a rescuer standing over his friend's lifeless body.

A stark realization hits him: "I've survived, but I'm stepping into a drastically altered world."

Doctors and nurses quickly discover the greatest risk to Jamie Andrew's survival: His hands and feet are so severely frostbitten that they are frozen solid. Once it's determined that the appendages are too damaged to be saved, he undergoes a quadruple amputation—the removal of both hands and both feet.

Waking up to bandaged stumps, Jamie lies in bed,

grappling with unimaginable grief, darkness, anger, and confusion. To emerge from this abyss, he embarks on a quest to understand the "why" of his tragedy and finds a glimmer of hope. *I am the fortunate one with a second chance at life.*

To honor his friend's bravery and courage, Jamie decides to rebuild his life one small task at a time.

Today, someone else brushed my teeth. Tomorrow, I'm going to brush my own teeth, he tells himself.

Every new task is yet another mountain to conquer.

Within weeks, Jamie is fitted with prosthetic limbs, and it isn't long before he takes his first step. Drawing on his natural athleticism, he takes up new sports — skiing, snowboarding, paragliding, and rock climbing — and he even returns to the Alps to summit the Matterhorn.

As he travels the world as a motivational speaker, raising thousands of dollars for charity, his mantra is clear: "I owe it to Jamie [Fisher] and his memory to make the most of this second chance and to see what's possible without hands and feet."

Disruptions Abound

We are currently living in an "age of disruption" amid exceptionally rapid changes that some of us are still coming to terms with and figuring out how to navigate.

Jamie Andrew's story powerfully illustrates life's inherent unpredictability and the sudden changes it can bring. Before his devastating incident, he was living life on his terms, enjoying adventure, camaraderie, and the raw beauty of nature. He was conquering both the literal and the symbolic mountains before him. Then, without warning, a life-altering event flipped his world upside down, challenging him to redefine what it means to live well and to pursue the good life once more on his terms.

While your experiences are unlikely to mirror Jamie's, disruptions in your life are as sure as the sun rising each day. They are universal. They come in various forms and vary in magnitude. Some disruptions, such as embarking on a new career path and navigating the conclusion of a relationship, are specific to you. Others affect everyone. These include global occurrences such as a pandemic and dramatic technological innovations, both of which can entirely transform the landscape for all.

Think of life's disruptions as curveballs—they're unexpected, often jarring, and can derail your carefully laid plans. They might sneak up on you quietly or hit you with the intensity of a snowstorm. Each disruption, whether personal or global, possesses the potential to either nudge you off your good-life path or guide you closer to your true aspirations. It's not the occurrence of these disruptions that's critical but rather how you respond to them.

Think of Jamie Andrew — he chose to take control of one new task each day, slowly moving over time from a life dependent on others to a rich life of interdependence. He teaches that every disruption, even the unthinkable, brings a choice. You can use it as an opportunity to shift your mindset, alter your course, and improve your outcomes. It's a chance to either inch closer to the life you envision or drift away from it.

Break down the word *disrupter:*

Disruption
Insights
Situation
Results
Use
Plan
Tell
Execute
Refine

- **Disruption:** Whether it's a sudden change, an ongoing trend, an unexpected incident, or a crisis, what is the specific issue you're experiencing?

- **Insights:** Observe how disruption changes the landscape of your environment, industry, or situation.
- **Situation:** Assess the challenges you are facing—and the strengths you possess to help you navigate the situation effectively.
- **Results:** Specify the results you aim to achieve, making a clear distinction between your current status and your desired goals.
- **Use:** What practical steps and actions can you leverage, and how do you plan to implement them?
- **Plan:** Create a detailed action plan and explain how each step will be carried out.
- **Tell:** Find the best way to reach out and share your message with others.
- **Execute:** Form a team, track your progress—and make adjustments as needed.
- **Refine:** Note what works well and what doesn't, and consider how to improve future actions and plans.

Positive Versus Negative Disrupters

In the face of disruption, you can be either a positive disrupter, one who seizes the opportunity for growth, innovation, and leadership, or a negative disrupter, one who dismisses or ignores change in an attempt to cling to something that no longer exists.

Positive disrupters see challenges as opportunities to grow. They often ask, "What can I learn from this situation?" Or they might say, "Let's explore new ways to solve this." Their actions lead others toward innovative solutions and along unexpected paths. They embrace change rather than fear it.

Conversely, negative disrupters favor resistance, often for resistance's sake. They introduce chaos and stubbornly adhere to outdated practices. Their opposition isn't rooted in a thoughtful critique of a situation but in an outright refusal to entertain new ideas. They are quick to dismiss innovations with statements such as "This change is unnecessary, and it won't work." Or they might resort to the age-old refrain "We've always done it this way!" While their skepticism might be warranted, their lack of openness to new possibilities is problematic. Their behavior isn't driven by a constructive or collaborative spirit but rather by a self-serving, sometimes destructive attitude.

Such individuals often cast a gloom over their environment, making it difficult for others to flourish around them. Their relationships struggle. Their families suffer. When they enter a room, their coworkers roll their eyes. Indeed, they bring disruption, but they lack any semblance of purpose, perspective, or productivity. Interacting with someone who consistently takes such a negative stance is exceedingly taxing on everyone in their midst.

Choosing to be a positive disrupter might seem foreign to some. It feels like a role reserved for others—a chosen few with big titles and bigger aspirations. But as you'll soon learn, being a positive disrupter is critical to having a good life, building a strong family, and growing a healthy work team or organization. And it's well within your grasp.

Which leads to **Fact 2: You're Wired to Disrupt.**

~~~~~~~~~~~~~~~~~~~~~~~~~~~~~~~~~~~~

Positive Disrupter Move

Own the Win

Give yourself credit today. Even if it's small. Especially if it is.

~~~~~~~~~~~~~~~~~~~~~~~~~~~~~~~~~~~~

Chapter 4
Fact 2: You're Wired to Disrupt

Keep the ideas coming.

In a small New York City apartment, a grocery store manager and a social worker raise ten children, five boys and five girls. More than half of them grow up to have notable careers in Hollywood. Among their most successful projects are family collaborations. Their last name is Wayans.

As the youngest child in a large family, Marlon Wayans has many teachers. His mother imparts her artistic sensibilities. His father demonstrates an unwavering commitment to hard work. "We called my dad an entre-poor-neur," Marlon jokes.

Rough-and-tumble childhood scuffles with his brothers teach him how to manage conflict—and laugh about it. Laughter is also a coping technique for loss.

"The worst thing happens, and the first thing we'd think is *What's funny about it?*" Marlon says. "I remember when my cousin Ceddy died and my auntie buried him in jeans and a T-shirt and some Air Force 1s and a baseball cap. Damon looks and goes, 'If there's a dress code in heaven, I don't think Ceddy's getting in.'"

As Damon, Shawn, and Keenen Ivory Wayans build comedy and film careers, Marlon begins his own formal training, successfully auditioning for admission to the famous Fiorello H. LaGuardia High School of Music & Art and Performing Arts.

"It's tough to be a Black hero" is the tagline of *I'm Gonna Git You Sucka*. The movie — directed, written by, and starring Marlon's older brother Keenen Ivory Wayans — is a parody of blaxploitation films of the 1970s. It's also sixteen-year-old Marlon's first film role.

After Marlon spends two years at Howard University, the pull of Hollywood becomes too strong to resist. He joins the cast of the TV comedy-variety show *In Living Color,* alongside Jamie Foxx, Jim Carrey, David Alan Grier, Chris Rock — and Wayans siblings Kim, Shawn, Keenen Ivory, and Damon.

"Don't just wait around for roles," Marlon's brother Keenen Ivory tells him. "Go out and create them."

This small piece of advice could easily have been overlooked. Sometimes a few words from a voice that matters to you can be all the disruption you need.

Marlon and his brother Shawn land *The Wayans Bros.,* the very first show to air on Warner Bros.' youth-centered network, the WB.

"We were 21 & 23 year old kids from the projects of Manhattan that created, exec produced, and starred in our very own sitcom," Marlon writes on Instagram. "We were fearless, young, crazy, funny, physical, edgy and free. We got skewered by critics, attacked by elders and often attacked by groups. Shawn and I never caved. We kept it real. We did it for the audience."

The show is a breakout success.

Connecting on a personal level becomes a continual touchpoint for Marlon, who says, "My goal is to bring laughter and a slice of joy to people, especially during their hardest moments."

The ideas keep coming. Marlon reteams with Shawn and Keenen to create, write, and star in a spoof of the horror genre, *Scary Movie,* and its sequel, *Scary Movie 2,* the bedrocks of a blockbuster franchise.

Marlon showcases his early training as a dramatic actor with his acclaimed portrayal of fictional heroin addict Tyrone C. Love in *Requiem for a Dream.* He also takes on reality-based roles—Aretha Franklin's ex-husband and manager, Ted White, in the biopic *Respect;* basketball player and coach turned Nike adviser George Raveling in *Air,* the story of the creation of Air Jordan sneakers.

He always returns to comedy, in television specials and live stand-up tours.

"This is a family recipe that we've had," he says of his natural ability to make people laugh. "You can't replicate what we do. You can have all the seasonings. You don't know how much to put on it."

The Hidden Truth About Disrupters

You may think, "That's great for Marlon Wayans, but he's a famous creative. I'm not." But being a positive disrupter isn't reserved for gifted actors and performers.

Let's turn the lens toward you.

Don't sell yourself short. Just like Marlon, you're wired to disrupt in three areas:

1. your brain
2. your experiences
3. your resources

1. Your Brain

You are meant to take risks, question the norm, and bring forth new ideas, no matter how outrageous they seem. Without this innate ability for innovative think-ing and action, the human race would not be even close to where it is today. We would most likely still be living in a world with no technology, inefficient transportation, and nothing nearly as good to eat as whatever you had for dinner last night.

Disruption is good.

Disruption is vital.

Disruption exists naturally within you.

You stand out in the animal kingdom, thanks to your unique ability to envision a future different from the present and intentionally take action to close the gap. This superpower comes from your prefrontal cortex, the brain's master planner. It handles every step of thinking and decision-making, thereby shaping your future and integrating information gleaned from what you see, hear, and remember. It's the place in the brain where you learn from associations, control your behavior based on rewards, make choices, and guide actions. Essentially, the prefrontal cortex is your brain's executive suite, predicting outcomes and coordinating complex plans.

The prefrontal cortex manages disruptive behavior through its three main sections.

The *medial* prefrontal cortex acts as your brain's coach, directing attention and motivation. It integrates information for decision-making, which is critical for pursuing significant life changes.

The *orbital and lateral* sections handle impulse control, emotional regulation, and the execution of disruptive ideas. The orbital prefrontal cortex aligns actions with goals and values, maintaining self-identity and relationships; the lateral prefrontal cortex is the command center for planning, cognitive flexibility, and working memory, enabling creative problem-solving and adaptation.

This isn't a neuroscience book, and there won't be an exam. Just know that your brain has remarkable capabilities that encourage you to tackle challenges, foster growth, and continually evolve.

2. Your Experiences

The disrupter and the disrupted are two universal roles in life. You might recall an instance akin to Marlon's experience, in which powerful advice resonated deeply, prompting a pivotal shift in your perspective or actions. It's possible you've altered your path, adopted new practices, transitioned between careers, or ventured to new locales—whether the next neighborhood or across the globe. You've probably spearheaded initiatives, introduced innovations to your team, adjusted your daily rituals, or navigated difficult situations among your family, friends, and coworkers. Each of these instances underscores your role as an agent of disruption.

Positive disrupter stories are punctuated with achievements that stand as beacons of adaptability and tenacity. These victories, whether grand or modest, comprise a record of ability to envision goals, face challenges, and triumph over those challenges. They bear witness to enduring spirit, ingenuity, and capacity to solve problems, bolstering self-assurance and propelling individuals forward. Armed with the knowledge of past successes, you're equipped to leap over future hurdles with the assurance that you have prevailed before and can undoubtedly do so again.

Whenever you're uncertain or questioning your readiness for a new challenge, pause to reflect on your past achievements. Document these successes, reflect on the effort you've invested, and let this inspire you. It's akin to giving yourself a motivational talk, reminding you of your past accomplishments and preparing you for future achievements. This process of self-affirmation is about reinforcing a belief in your capabilities, assuring yourself, "I can handle this." Given your track record, there's no limit to what you can achieve next.

Positive Disrupter Move

Check Your Receipts

Remind yourself: *You've done hard things before.* Name one obstacle you've crushed, one disruption you survived. Concrete proof. You're built for this.

Ready to explore what you can learn from your experiences? Check out "Tool 3: Tap into Your Experience" in Part VII.

~~~~~~

Although reflecting on your life experiences offers valuable insights into your capabilities and resilience, consider a note of caution. Experience, though informative and uplifting, can sometimes be deceptive. Reviewing your achievements can fuel motivation, inspire you, and affirm your potential. Yet it's crucial to recognize that the strategies and solutions that succeeded in the past aren't guaranteed to yield the same results in the future.

Life is dynamic. New situations will arise, requiring new approaches. So while drawing on past experiences for confidence and guidance is beneficial, it's essential to avoid viewing them as a precise blueprint for future actions.

Think of your past experiences as a toolkit rather than a script: They equip you with skills and insights, but creativity and adaptability are key in applying them to new contexts. Let your past victories inspire you, but remain open to innovation and the use of new strategies for navigating the ever-evolving landscape of life's challenges.

3. Your Resources

As you pursue your good life, remember that you have a treasure trove of resources to tap into. Technology, for example, ranges from simple gadgets that you use daily to sophisticated software that can revolutionize the way you work. While sometimes seeming sparse, financial resources can stretch far with smart management and strategic planning. The realm of knowledge, accessible through books, online courses, and tutorials, is vast and ever-expanding, offering insights and guidance for virtually any endeavor.

Take a moment to consider how you could more effectively use the resources at your disposal. Explore the untapped opportunities surrounding you and consult with others to uncover resources you might not have initially recognized. You probably have team members or family members with different experiences and talents who can collaborate with you on disruptive ideas to create something amazing.

The Choice Is Yours

Indeed, you're not Marlon Wayans — and that's perfectly fine.

You are uniquely you.

Embrace that individuality and choose to engage

proactively with the disruptions in your world to carve out your version of a good life.

But first, a word of caution.

You can come to grips with the first two facts: Disruptions are part of life, and you possess the ability to turn these challenges into something positive. Yet you still find yourself hesitating to take action.

Why is that? For starters, you may resist changes that are barreling toward you at full speed. You dig in, look the other way, and hope to outlast the chaos. But that kind of mindset can put you at a disadvantage—leaving you feeling lost, cheated, and downright frustrated.

Furthermore, the path of a positive disrupter is undeniably demanding. Those who choose it (and their teams and organizations) will often be met with criticism. And success is never guaranteed.

Thankfully, you are not alone.

Relationships can kick-start your thinking, build on your experiences, and help you get things moving. When you share your vision with others, you're not only talking about your goals—you're also opening doors to collaboration and support that might otherwise remain closed.

Throughout this book, you'll encounter the stories of individuals who found inspiration and support through their relationships, forging partnerships that at times seemed to offer little promise but ultimately led to great achievements. The foundations of these success stories are always the same: a clear vision, a passionate drive, relentless effort, and the courage to build and invest in relationships.

Think about your own network—your friends, family, colleagues, and even those old acquaintances. These connections are a treasure trove of advice, support, and opportunities. The wisdom from mentors and the support from peers who share your journey or have been there before can be incredibly comforting and enlightening.

Never forget that relationships are more than just a means to an end; they are also a vital part of the richness of life itself. The connections you forge and maintain contribute deeply to your personal fulfillment and happiness, making journeys not only successful but also meaningful. This leads to **Fact 3: Relationships Provide Headwinds and Tailwinds.**

Positive Disrupter Move

See What's in Your Hands

When life feels tight, stop. Name three resources you have: skills, people, tools, time. You're not empty-handed. You've got what you need to start.

Not sure what resources you have available? Check out "Tool 4: Inventory Your Resources" in Part VII.

Chapter 5

Fact 3: Relationships Provide Headwinds and Tailwinds

Don't go it alone. Build a first-rate support system around you and always rely on it.

"I entered this room, and there were drugs...I asked for some," Trina Frierson says.

She's emerged from that harrowing descent into a decade-long battle with addiction as the founding president and CEO of the nonprofit organization Mending Hearts. Based in West Nashville, Tennessee, the residential recovery program supports women struggling with addiction and homelessness.

Trina's transformed herself several times. Not always for the good.

"I was that kid who played every sport—basketball,

softball, track — you name it," she says, reminiscing about the abilities that earned her a college athletic scholarship.

During her sophomore year, she became pregnant, dropped out of college, and entered a toxic relationship.

Who first introduced her to drugs? Someone she trusted, who "slipped some cocaine into a cigarette, and just like that, I was down the rabbit hole," she recounts.

Escaping the "old playground" of relationships and harmful environments that enabled drug use seemed impossible. It wasn't until her third stay in a transitional home, surrounded by a supportive community, that she found the stability she needed to recover.

"The only reason I made it this time was because of the incredible support system I had around me," she says.

"We talk about the therapeutic value of one addict helping another, and I think that house did it for me," Trina recalls. "There were women just like me who'd suffered as well. These women were not only coming from incarceration but had tried the process of recovery. In that process of recovery, they showed me the ins and outs of how to live. And in that process, I remember women calling me and asking me, 'Trina, are you really clean? How are you doing this?' And I was able to tell them about the great support that I'd had, you know, with women empowering women."

Motivated by her own final release from incarceration, Trina committed herself to deep reflection and prayer and made a solemn vow: to stay sober and dedicate her life to helping other women escape the clutches of addiction.

"We need to have a resource center, so when women come out of incarceration," Trina says, "they are able to stop at this hub, to get the resources that they need, to be edified to be a member of society. And so that was the dream."

To create Mending Hearts, Trina follows a theory of psychological motivation called Maslow's hierarchy of needs. From most basic to most elevated, they are: physiological needs (such as food, clothing, and shelter); the need for safety; the need for love and belonging; the need for self-esteem; and the need for self-actualization. Fulfilling the most basic needs allows the one above it to be met; and in turn the next one, and so on.

"I couldn't have done any of this on my own," Trina says of building Mending Hearts, which has reached its full capacity of serving 110 women at a time. Since its inception, in 2004, more than five thousand women have received the benefits of the therapeutic program. The success stories transcend statistics.

"Living together, these women foster a culture of accountability," Trina notes of the neighborhood redevelopment program that turns "dope houses" into "houses of hope."

As Trina builds connections across community lines—from local churches to the corridors of city hall—she notes, "I've formed relationships with mayors, councils, senators." Through connections once thought unattainable, she's created "the largest female, full-team care service provider in the state of Tennessee."

Life Is a Team Sport

Trina's story shows us that strong relationships are like a steady wind at your back, guiding you toward your goals and enriching your life. They are valuable not just as a means to an end but also as a big part of the end itself.

On the other hand, poor relationships are like a relentless headwind, hindering progress and making every effort feel more arduous than it needs to be. These relationships act as invisible anchors, holding you back. They can be relationships you've neglected; they might have been strong once but have been allowed to wither or decline through lack of attention. Headwinds may also come in the form of relationships that should never have been established in the first place. You might know they aren't serving you well, but they persist nonetheless.

Living a good life really comes down to the relationships you nurture. They enrich life and make it fulfilling. Challenge yourself to take a hard look at your relationships. It's about strengthening the ones that need a little help and having the courage to let go of the ones that hold you back. Yes, it's tough, but it's also crucial for your growth.

So are the tailwind relationships in your life — those special bonds that push you forward, lift you up during tough times, and cheer you on when you succeed.

Positive disrupters know that life is a team sport.

They've shown that achieving big goals, bouncing back from setbacks, and simply finding joy are rarely solo journeys. By focusing on building up those around you, you create a network that supports you and shares in both your challenges and your victories. You're setting yourself up for a truly rewarding life.

In Trina's journey, relationships have played pivotal roles, acting as both headwinds and tailwinds.

The most striking examples of headwinds come from the very beginning of Trina's addiction — the people who first exposed her to drugs. Those relationships pushed her deeper into addiction, making each step toward recovery more difficult. There were also people in Trina's life who, while not directly contributing to her drug use, stood by silently as she suffered. These invisible anchors watched her struggle without intervention; some may have even derived quiet satisfaction from her troubles. These relationships weighed her down, making her feel isolated and unsupported during her darkest times.

On the flip side, the supportive community in the transitional home acted as a powerful tailwind for Trina. These individuals shared everything with her—from their meals to their personal struggles—helping her break down numerous barriers. What's more, the relationships she cultivated through Mending Hearts, helping other women overcome their addictions, continue to propel her forward.

Take a proactive approach to your relationships. Engaging positively with others doesn't just make your life better; it also makes it worth living.

Consider the people closest to you in your daily life:

Your team leaders—Do you feel they are holding you back... or are they actually trying to help you and teach you?

Your team members—Do you see them as merely a means to get what you need... or are they fellow humans whose well-being you care about?

And how about **your family?**—Do you focus on their annoying behaviors... or on all the various attributes that make them interesting?

Remember that managing your relationships isn't just about dealing with the difficult ones. It's also about celebrating and strengthening those that bring you joy and help you soar.

Which leads to **Fact 4: Your Time Here Is Finite—Make It Count in Ways That Matter.**

Positive Disruptive Move

Be Someone's Tailwind Today

Relationships either lift you up or hold you down. Today, pick one person and give them a boost—a text, a compliment, a helping hand. Make it easier for them to fly.

Are you ready to assess your relationships? Turn to "Tool 5: Analyze Your Relationships" in Part VII.

Chapter 6

Fact 4: Your Time Here Is Finite — Make It Count in Ways That Matter

True fulfillment can be found along the most unexpected paths.

"What would your twenty-two-year-old self say if he saw you sitting here in this car wash?"

Tom D'Eri, cofounder and COO of Rising Tide Car Wash, answers without hesitation. "He'd say I'm exactly where I'm supposed to be."

The successful South Florida business cleans more than 150,000 cars annually, but its origin story is about taking care of family.

Entrepreneur John D'Eri raises his two sons, Tom and Andrew, on practical advice. "There is no magic, just hard work." When Tom graduates from college with a business degree, that means identifying and pursuing a rewarding career.

It's a little trickier for his brother, Andrew, then about to graduate from high school. He possesses excellent attention to detail and enjoys tasks that follow a consistent routine, yet there's no denying that his professional prospects are grim. Andrew faces a daunting statistic that's widely reported: 85 percent of people like him, on the autism spectrum, are unemployed.

A D'Eri family goal emerges — creating a business that could not only employ Andrew but create a community for him as well. A business "purposefully built to empower individuals with autism," says Tom. "So we set the goal of employing people with autism for 80 percent of our staff."

The family decides that car washing fits the bill, and they spend a summer studying the necessary logistics and other details. The result is Rising Tide Car Wash.

In the early days, like any new business, Rising Tide faces the stress and strain of designing workable systems, meeting customer expectations, and turning a profit. Their dedication to employing a workforce of people on the autism spectrum adds several degrees of difficulty, however.

Tom faces a recurring scenario: customers' appreciation of Rising Tide's social mission often collides with their primary concern — getting their cars cleaned. Misunderstandings escalate quickly, putting pressure on Tom to defuse tense situations. His problem-solving abilities run up against a steep learning curve, with the entire future of the business at stake. All he wants is "to get to the end of the day, when I could put my head on the pillow before starting all over again the next day."

He finds himself questioning his decisions, wondering if he's chosen the wrong line of work. This introspection leads him to a pivotal realization. Regardless of any business problems, Tom's underlying motivation — to support his brother — remains constant.

Sticking to this goal makes Tom a positive disrupter.

He realizes that it's not about doing something special to make his business function, but learning how to solve fundamental business problems through a different lens, to make it more functional *for his employees.* "This means understanding that people with autism may have different ways of thinking and processing information and adapting to their needs. By doing so, we can create a more inclusive and diverse workforce," Tom says.

Tom D'Eri would be the first to tell you he's just a regular guy. But he chose to embrace change in one disruptive moment and seek stability in another. When faced with the daily challenges of running the car wash, Tom chose stability by doubling down on his efforts to make the business successful, rather than closing the shop and walking away. He realized that grounding himself in the moment was the best way to fuel the fire inside.

Rising Tide now stands out as one of the busiest car washes in Florida, boasting an employee retention rate five times higher than its competitors' and revenues that far exceed industry standards. The D'Eri family also launch Rising Tide U, to help other people interested in building autism-friendly businesses. Rising Tide Car Wash has successfully expanded to three locations that in total employ more than ninety employees on the autism spectrum—all of whom are pursuing their own good lives.

Positive Disrupter Move

Control Your Zone

Let go of what's out there. Focus on your choices, your energy, your lane.

Quick Recap:
Fire, Fuel, and Four Facts

To live your good life, dare to define your terms:

What makes the fire burn inside you?
How can you throw fuel on that fire?
How can you disrupt beyond yourself?

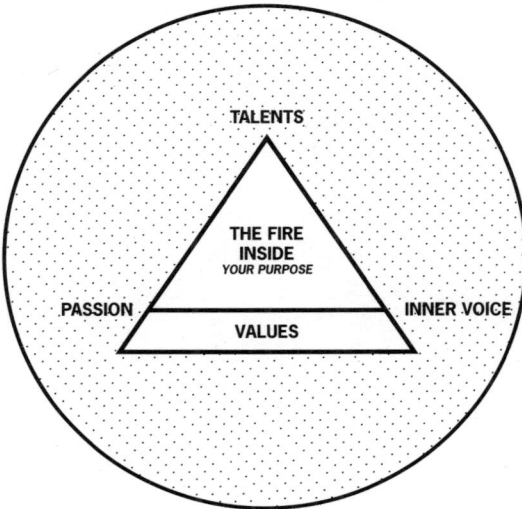

TALENTS

THE FIRE
INSIDE
YOUR PURPOSE

PASSION

VALUES

INNER VOICE

Disrupting Beyond Yourself:

These actions don't merely apply to you as an individual—they're also about your family, your team, and your entire organization.

Each person, each group, each family—they all have a purpose, just like you. And they all operate under the same four fundamental facts.

Four foundational facts can help you move closer to or further away from achieving your good life:

Fact 1: The status quo is a deceptive little devil

Life naturally brings changes and surprises.
These changes can help or hinder your journey.

Fact 2: You're wired to disrupt

Your brain is prewired for disruption.
Your experiences are valuable.
Your resources are abundant.

Fact 3: Relationships provide headwinds and tailwinds

Relationships provide richness to life.
Relationships can be either headwinds holding
    you back or tailwinds pushing you forward.

Fact 4: Your Time Here Is Finite — Make It Count in Ways That Matter

Choose to be a positive influence.
You get one life — make it count!

Part II
The Positive Disrupter Loop

Chapter 7

Disruption on the Streets of India

Progress comes from meeting people—and problems— where they live.

Pia Lindell Qwist has been working hard on starting a restaurant in Greve, Denmark, on the outskirts of Copenhagen. She's invested most of her money in her new business, saving just enough to vacation with friends in New Delhi, India.

The group has hired a driver to guide them through the unfamiliar city. As the vehicle weaves its way through the crowded streets, Pia asks the driver to pull over.

Instead of drawing the breath of fresh air she's craving, Pia finds herself breathless with shock at the condition of the two young children who approach her with outstretched hands. They appear to be siblings between the ages of three and five.

Their eyes are empty—as if they have given up.

She steps back into the car, reeling with sadness and concern.

According to the driver, they are orphans. "People do whatever they want with street children and then discard them," he says with apparent indifference.

Pia confronts the injustice of the situation. She's a visitor in this city, soon to return to a comfortable life in Denmark, while these children have no relief from their brutal existence.

She insists that the driver show her where the street children live.

The car stops under a bridge. The scant shelter provides some protection from the elements but none from the grime that covers everything and everyone beneath it.

Many children, some as young as two and three years old, huddle around the fire they keep burning to warm the cold air. Like the two children who approached Pia in the street, they are hesitant and afraid, nothing like the young ones she knows back home.

The driver makes a second stop at a small train station, where children are sleeping on the dirty floor.

"The children went directly into my heart," Pia says. "I couldn't let go of them. I see their eyes, their bodies, those two children; this doesn't seem right. They did not decide to be there. They have not asked to do it. And now they're standing there with nothing. There's something totally wrong with the situation."

On the flight home, Pia asks herself two questions:

How can children live under such conditions?
What can I do to help them?

As an individual, she faces many obstacles. Her lack of knowledge about child welfare practices in India. The 3,500 miles that separate Copenhagen and New Delhi. A lack of financial backers.

Yet four months later, she's still haunted by the memories of the children who held out their hands for help.

As a restaurateur, she makes conversation with people throughout the day. Mentions of the children's plight provoke as many dismissive responses as encouraging ones.

Hospitalized for a medical procedure, she encounters a fellow patient who offers simple, powerful advice. "Listen to me, please," the old woman says as she stares directly into Pia's eyes. "Follow your heart. All those making bad noise, put them away and go where your heart is."

These words strengthen Pia's resolve. She considers tapping into her network of fellow business owners to raise funds and reaching out to nongovernmental organizations (NGOs) for guidance. She's frustrated to learn that NGOs are more interested in making financial contributions than giving the hands-on support she yearns to offer.

Following a mentor's advice, she takes time away from her business and her young family to make a solo trip to Kolkata, India, another city where impoverished children live under bridges, in parking lots, and at train stations. To fulfill her commitment to making a tangible difference in their lives, Pia begins splitting her time between Denmark and India.

People at home are often critical, questioning Pia's motivations for making these trips and subjecting herself to disappointment and heartache.

"At first, the street children were wary of me," Pia says. They would steal from her, but she made sure to never carry more money than she could afford to lose. Despite having her wallet and handbag stolen several times, Pia empathizes with the children and never responds out of anger. "I understood why they did it. If I were in their shoes, struggling for food on the streets, I might do the same." Her patience and understanding eventually pay off.

"After about nine or ten visits, something changed. One evening, about ten or twelve kids approached me, asking why I kept returning despite their thefts. I told them I cared about them and wanted to help, but I needed their input and trust to really make a difference."

It's the breakthrough she's been hoping for. "Once they accepted me, it was complete," Pia says. "They knew the streets better than anyone and even protected me in several situations. We started making real progress, and that was a huge gift. I promised them I would never let them down."

The children begin opening up to Pia about their lives and experiences, their hopes and dreams. "When I asked them their biggest wishes," Pia says, "three things were consistent: daily meals, education, and a home."

The children's wishes became the basis for Pia's organization, Gadens Børn—Danish for "street children."

Funded largely by support from Danish businesses and operated by volunteers and staff based in both Copenhagen and Kolkata, Gadens Børn feeds, educates, and provides medical care to children in need.

"In 2012, I went on a trip to India with my girlfriends," Pia says. "It should have been a normal holiday, but what we saw and experienced there changed my life."

Within its first seven years, Gadens Børn changes the lives of hundreds of children in Kolkata by establishing three schools, a recreation center, a mobile health clinic, and even a facility for mothers and babies.

Since then, Pia's organization has gone on to open another medical clinic, four more activity centers, a girls' home, and a boarding school.

Over lunch in a Copenhagen café, Pia outlines the ongoing commitment of the Gadens Børn team. "We fight for our cause every day, and although some cases are tougher than others, we have no intention of giving up on them. We've seen the difference we can make, time and time again, and we're not stopping anytime soon."

Chapter 8
The Positive Disrupter Loop

Disrupt. Discern. Behave. Achieve. Refine.

While the Positive Disrupter Loop is not the *only* way to initiate a disruption or cope with one, it's often the most effective way.

Positive disrupters such as Pia Lindell Qwist illustrate the power of the Positive Disrupter Loop:

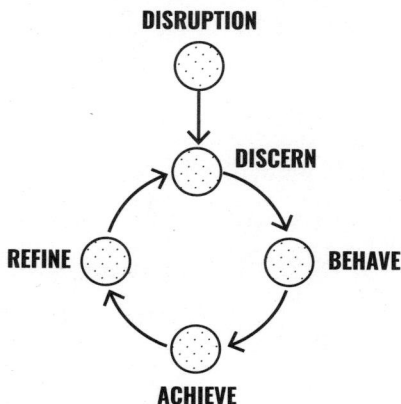

DISRUPTION

DISCERN

REFINE

BEHAVE

ACHIEVE

The loop consists of five steps.

Step 1: Disrupt—The Positive Disrupter Loop begins with some change to your life, your relationships, your family, or your work. This change will be significant to you or your team, whether or not it seems significant to anyone else.

Step 2: Discern—Every disruption has the potential to shape your thought processes, either by reinforcing your existing beliefs or by prompting you to adopt a new viewpoint. These shifts in thinking are deeply rooted in your purpose, values, and relationships. The Discern step challenges you to be aware of the shifts and proactively choose how you will respond in each situation.

Step 3: Behave—Changes in mindsets pave the way for new behaviors, routines, and habits. If you want to improve a situation, you can't just *think* differently; you've also got to *act* differently. Making some small behavioral changes—spending more quality time with your family, gathering more feedback from your customers, upping your hours at the gym—can all have a remarkable impact.

Step 4: Achieve—As you behave in new ways, you get new results. Quantify your outcomes across your various relationships and roles to track your achievements. Some may be positive, some negative, or perhaps a mix of both.

Step 5: Refine—The crucial Refine step challenges you to review your results, reflect on what they mean, revise your expectations or approach, and recommit yourself to future efforts.

Let's use Pia's story to further explore the Positive Disrupter Loop.

Step 1: Disrupt

Pia's encounter with street children in India is a profound example of how disruptions can fuel the fire inside. Initially in tourist mode with her friends, she shifted her perspective dramatically when she saw the children's vacant eyes, reflecting their harsh living conditions. This, coupled with the driver's indifferent reaction, created a stark contrast to Pia's life in Denmark. It also ignited her inherent empathy and desire to help.

Step 2: Discern

Pia's curiosity about the children's story, especially in the context of the driver's indifference, led to a deeper questioning of her purpose and an attempt to decipher social norms. Where many might see an unfortunate but unchangeable aspect of local life, Pia saw something unacceptable and needing change. It ignited the fire inside. This perspective is at the heart of what it means to think differently in the face of disruption. It entails recognizing problems and feeling a personal responsibility to solve them.

Disruptions can be powerful catalysts for change, prompting you to reevaluate your perspectives and question your choices. Most important, they inspire action. This is the essence of a mindset shift: seeing the world differently and being motivated to do something about it. In Pia's case, it encouraged her to change from a passive observer into an active participant in the quest for a better life for the children.

Step 3: Behave

Pia's experience teaches that when your mindset shifts in alignment with your values and purpose, you are propelled into action, even when the road ahead is uncertain. When you are moved by something greater than yourself, you can overcome incredible odds to make a positive difference in the world.

Her story also underscores the significance of acting with patience and empathy when trying to bring about change and achieve new results: understanding difficult circumstances, using an approach not of frustration or judgment but of deep sensitivity. Building trust and relationships, especially in challenging environments, requires time, patience, and a genuine effort to understand the perspective of the people you're trying to help.

In addition, Pia's story highlights the value of persistence. Despite slow progress and initial setbacks, her consistent efforts and repeated visits eventually led to a breakthrough. This persistence in the face of challenges is a critical lesson, showing that perseverance is crucial to achieving long-term goals, especially in situations that change hearts and minds.

Notably, Pia's strategy was characterized by working at a pace appropriate for the children's situation. She understood the importance of not rushing to impose solutions but taking the time to understand their needs and earn their trust. This lesson is vital not only in outreach and aid work but also in every endeavor in which the pace of progress must be matched to that of the people you are looking to work with and serve.

Step 4: Achieve

In two years, with consistent and persistent action, Pia's efforts yielded several achievements—mutual trust, shared understanding, and a willingness on the children's part to share their biggest wishes. Pia showed them what love in action looks like.

Her efforts influenced others to join the mission of Gadens Børn. As her vision for what was possible grew, this shift from individual effort to a collective approach allowed her to make a more significant and lasting impact. She then took her efforts even further by expanding her team and partnering with businesses—not just for fundraising and in-kind donations but also to create ambassadors like fellow Danish businesswoman Kristine Emery Ruglykke.

Kristine, the Sales and Product Manager at Danish clothing brand MSCH Copenhagen, was inspired by the mission after getting a request to donate T-shirts. "[Pia's] love for these children and her persistent fight to provide them with a dignified life made a significant impression on me," Kristine says. "I visited Pia in Kolkata and witnessed firsthand the tremendous difference she and the dedicated staff of Gadens Børn make for so many vulnerable children. It put things into perspective for me, and I decided to engage further."

Step 5: Refine

The Positive Disrupter Loop doesn't conclude with achievements; it progresses into a crucial refinement phase. In this stage, positive disrupters thoughtfully review outcomes, reflect on successes and setbacks, revise their approaches, and renew their commitments. This vital step can be easily overlooked and underestimated. Don't fall into this trap — refinement is essential for long-term sustainable progress.

Let's look at how Pia effectively engaged the Refine step, exemplifying its importance in the loop. Her reflection on her initial two years in India showed a significant transition from mistrust to trust, marking her evolution from an outsider to an advocate. This deep introspection made her realize the importance of collaborative efforts. Acting on these insights, she shifted her focus from direct aid to establishing Gadens Børn, a structured initiative providing meals, education, and a safe environment — a move toward a sustainable approach. Despite numerous challenges, Pia's unwavering commitment to the children of Kolkata only grew stronger with each visit. As a result, Gadens Børn's success led to lessons learned, new goals established, and further results achieved.

Quick Recap: The Positive Disrupter Loop

The Positive Disrupter Loop helps ordinary people transform their careers, families, teams, products, businesses, and more.

Outstanding leaders and disrupters like Pia act on the five steps intuitively, just by following their own instincts. Fortunately, the rest of us can follow their examples to figure out what to focus on at each step of the process.

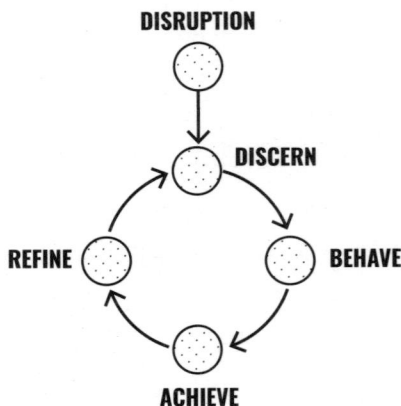

Part III
Discern

Chapter 9
The Power of Discernment

See a life of potential, not of limitations.

"I will start by saying that my disability is kind of at the center of my story," Mindy Henderson states. "That's not to say there isn't more to me than my disability, but it has played a central and significant role in shaping my life."

At only fifteen months old, Mindy received a medical diagnosis of spinal muscular atrophy. "Back then, there was very little known about this condition. It was rare. My parents were told I would lose my ability to stand and walk. I had started to stand and walk when babies normally do, but I stopped pretty quickly after that."

The doctors delivered the devastating news to Mindy's parents, who were only in their twenties at the time. "They were also told I would lose all of my cognitive function and probably wouldn't live to be three. As you can imagine, that's devastating news for any parent to get."

In the face of this prognosis, Mindy says, "my parents decided that if this was how the story was going to go, they wanted to know they had done absolutely everything they could for me."

Her father was a former collegiate athlete with a deep understanding of anatomy and physiology. He took a scientific approach. "He put together a plan, knowing what he knew about the body, to see if he and my mom could make some positive impact," Mindy explains, continuing, "I don't know if he had much confidence it would work, but he was determined to try."

Together, Mindy's parents embarked on a journey of relentless determination and hope. "They started with physical therapy. Little by little, I did start to get stronger," Mindy says. "The predictions of losing my cognitive function and not making it past my third birthday were proven to be untrue."

Both profound challenges and unexpected opportunities marked Mindy's childhood. From ages four to twelve, she served as a state ambassador for the Muscular Dystrophy Association. "I gave speeches at the age of four, which was very interesting," she says with a chuckle. "I told some really bad jokes back then, but those experiences taught me how to turn a negative into a positive. And it gave me the speaking bug."

Her journey has been one of defying expectations and embracing possibilities. "I lived a life full of what I saw as potential rather than limitations," Mindy says proudly. "I went to college, sang on national television and recorded music, earned a master's degree, had a twenty-year career in high tech, and eventually became a motivational speaker, author, and the vice president of disability, outreach & empowerment and editor in chief of Quest Media for the Muscular Dystrophy Association."

In their darkest moments, Mindy's parents chose hope, action, and unwavering support. They took the time to discern what they could do in the face of the disruptive diagnosis and determine the role they should play. Fueled by their example, Mindy, too, has chosen to embrace a role filled with hope and action.

Their decisions made all the difference.

Don't Just React—Discern

Living a good life requires more than just reacting hastily to every disruption that comes your way. Each disruption you experience, no matter how big or small, presents a critical opportunity, offering you the chance to move forward, hold back, strike out on your own, or collaborate with others. True success hinges on your ability to discern — to know when to embrace an opportunity and when to let it pass.

Positive disruption isn't about acting impulsively. It's about making informed decisions, driven by a clear sense of purpose and a readiness to take meaningful action. This often involves embracing change, but it can also mean seeking stability. In fact, choosing to step back in the face of disruption, especially when the crowd is whipped up into a frenzy over the latest new and shiny object, might be the most disruptive move you can make.

Avoiding knee-jerk reactions to every disruption and resisting the urge to wait indefinitely for the perfect moment is key. The true skill lies in knowing precisely how, when, and why to act.

Put simply, you must discern.

So how do you discern what to do in the face of disruption?

When encountering a disruption — whether it's a sudden opportunity, an unexpected change, or any event that interrupts your routine and demands your attention — you find yourself at a pivotal crossroads. At this juncture, you're faced with deciding if you should

(1) seek change or seek stability and (2) act independently or act collaboratively.

Choice 1: Seek Change or Seek Stability

Do you embrace change and venture in a new direction? Or do you prioritize stability by maintaining your current path or even returning to a well-worn trail? Choosing change involves adapting and venturing into the unknown, while opting for stability means upholding consistency and minimizing disruption.

Choice 2: Act Independently or Act Collaboratively

Should you tackle the situation on your own or work with others? This decision hinges on whether the circumstances call for solo efforts or a team effort.

Self-Awareness and Situational Awareness

Choosing the best way to navigate a disruption requires a balance between self-awareness — understanding your own wants and needs — and situational awareness, which involves recognizing what the situation requires you to do.

For example, imagine a former boss calling you and offering you a job in a different city with a significant salary increase and room for advancement at a respected organization. You might be flattered by the offer and excited about the opportunity. As you reflect on your career goals, your instinct might be to jump at the offer and the chance to change course, but it's crucial to weigh your desires and interests against other factors, such as family, friends, and ongoing commitments in your present location.

You might have children in school. You might have a spouse with their own career considerations. You might be involved in community activities or lead a critical project at work. These situations can complicate the decision, making it essential to think beyond your immediate desires and evaluate the broader impact on your life and the lives of those around you.

Deciding whether to accept such an offer involves discerning whether to seek change or stability and whether to act independently or collaboratively. You must consider how taking the job or turning it down might fuel the fire inside you or tamp down your internal flame.

Discussing the opportunity with your family and friends can provide crucial insights. Their reactions — whether excitement, reluctance, or curiosity — will inform your decision, helping you understand how your choices affect your relationships and your long-term goals. Ultimately, the decision to accept the new role or to decline it must be carefully considered. Each option has its merits, and determining the best choice requires a thoughtful evaluation of all factors.

Here's a more organization-oriented example. Imagine you're the leader of a chain of retail stores. Over the past twenty years, you've watched your competition move more and more online. It's not that you completely reject e-commerce — you know that it has a place in the retail landscape.

But you've always believed that your chain's core purpose is delivering amazing in-person experiences. You want your customers to feel good about spending time in your stores, turning shopping from a chore into a leisurely and enjoyable experience they can share with friends and family.

You think hard about whether or not to follow your competitors. You have a decision to make: double down on online shopping, maintaining revenue at the risk of transforming your stores into glorified warehouses? Or continue to focus on delivering a high-quality in-person experience for dwindling foot traffic?

Like Dick's Sporting Goods president and CEO Lauren Hobart has done, you conclude that you'll invest modestly in your online presence but continue to focus your investments on the in-store experience.

"We are creating an experience that people cannot

get anywhere else," Hobart says of her stores, which cater to active consumers—particularly their "House of Sport" locations, which include batting cages, climbing walls, and more. Dick's is now the largest sporting goods retail company in the United States, with more than 850 stores and still growing. "Athletes are really responding to it, so communities are responding to it.... Athletes are coming in, they're driving farther, they're spending more time, they're really excited about the product and the experience."

The Five Roles of a Positive Disrupter

There are five dynamic roles you can adopt during moments of disruption. By practicing self-reflection, maintaining situational awareness, seeking others' input, and staying true to your fire inside, you can effectively take on any one of these meaningful roles. It's important to remember that these roles are situational—they change depending on the circumstances. They aren't fixed archetypes or personality traits. Instead, choose the appropriate role for each situation, and as circumstances evolve, roles may switch. The key takeaway is that these roles are tools to help you achieve your good life. They define how you will act in a given situation, not who you are in every situation.

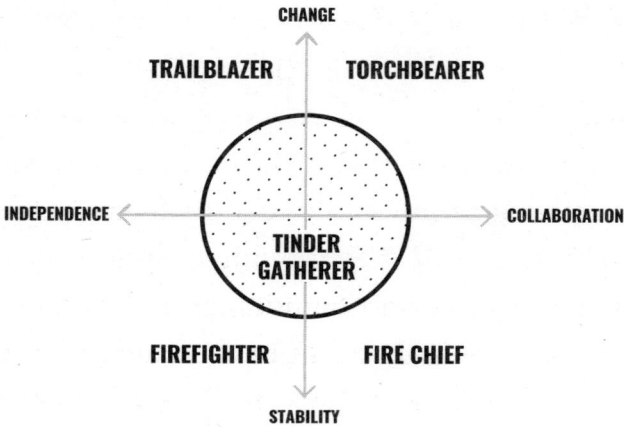

Since disruption can help you throw fuel on the fire inside, let's continue with the fire analogy. **Trailblazer, Firefighter, Torchbearer, Fire Chief,** and **Tinder Gatherer** are the five distinct roles that maximize engagement with disruption for yourself, your team, your organization, or your family.

1. *Trailblazer: Seek Change and Act Independently*

If you find yourself initiating change through individual efforts, the role of Trailblazer might be your path. To be a Trailblazer requires bold individual initiative, acting as a pioneer, clearing new paths, and breaking new ground. It includes stepping into intimidating changes such as switching jobs, going back to school, or urging your organization to try an untested idea.

2. *Firefighter:* Seek Stability and Act Independently

The role of Firefighter demands making decisive and sometimes unilateral decisions in order to manage and mitigate change, with a particular focus on how stability in the face of disruption can matter most in the long term. As a Firefighter, you'll work to contain disruptive situations and minimize their impact, ensuring that stability is maintained through calculated and prompt action. This doesn't mean that you lack innovation, creativity, or a desire to make a big impact — it's often the complete opposite.

3. *Torchbearer:* Seek Change and Act Collaboratively

As a Torchbearer, you aim to achieve change through collective action, leveraging the strengths and dynamics of a group. While you may lead the overall effort, the essence of your success lies in rallying others toward a shared goal. Torchbearers often start a movement with and through others.

4. *Fire Chief:* Seek Stability and Act Collaboratively

The Fire Chief works with and through others to address disruptions, recognizing that a movement *away* from chasing the latest opportunity might be the most disruptive choice in the moment.

5. *Tinder Gatherer: Pursue Clarity and Provide Support*

The Tinder Gatherer role offers a bit of a twist because it involves gathering essential information and assisting others. While some Tinder Gatherers eventually transition into one of the aforementioned roles, many remain in a supportive capacity. This role's flexibility allows you to support the disruptive efforts of other people while providing you with the opportunity for further discernment of your own.

Choosing the Right Role at the Right Time

The focus here is on discernment: thinking differently, recognizing opportunities amid disruption, assessing when change is necessary, and identifying who needs to be involved. This stage is critical: It requires navigating the tumultuous waters of disruption with a clear sense of purpose and a commitment to your values and relationships.

~~~~~~

Positive Disrupter Move

Pick Your Role

Ask yourself, "Am I leading? Supporting? Holding the line?" Give your day a job title.

Are you facing a disruption and aren't sure which role to play? Check out "Tool 6: Discern Your Ideal Role (for Now)" in Part VII.

~~~~~~

Chapter 10
Trailblazer: Seek Change and Act Independently

Seek a path that only you can tread.

In the 1960s, Josie Natori leaves the Philippines to attend school in the United States. Fast-forward a decade, and she is making a rapid ascent in the corporate world, becoming the first female vice president of investment banking at Merrill Lynch. In an era and industry dominated by men, Josie is more than a participant—she's a trailblazing, attention-getting pioneer.

There's just one problem with her widely admired finance career: for her, it simply isn't fulfilling.

Fueled by an entrepreneurial urge coupled with a desire to work in a creative field, Josie dares to make a leap into the unknown. She explores a range of opportunities, including opening a McDonald's franchise in Queens and a car wash in Manhattan, but those businesses, as she told us, didn't "touch me."

Once she focuses on her pride in her Filipina heritage, Josie's journey from the corridors of Wall Street to the runways of the fashion world begins.

In her living room, she cuts fabric, designing pieces of lingerie. She books appointments with New York City retailers, pitching a collarless Filipina-style tunic. Josie faces a barrage of rejections until she meets with a buyer at Bloomingdale's, who offers suggestions for modifying the garment into what later becomes an iconic sleep shirt.

She names her business the Natori Company. Collection after collection, Josie continues to produce variations on that original garment as she expands her offerings from lingerie and sleepwear into an East-meets-West clothing and lifestyle brand—including the luxury labels Josie Natori and Natori and additional lines like N Natori and Josie by Natori.

Key to her success have been the relationships she cultivated during her years on Wall Street—and those of her son, Ken Natori. In 2007, he leaves his own career in finance and television broadcasting to become president of Natori, initially focusing on e-commerce, supply-chain logistics, and hybrid retail.

Upon her 2022 induction into the Accessories

Council Hall of Fame, Josie says, "I am so honored by this incredible recognition of all we have done at Natori. My goal when I started forty-five years ago was to dress women from the inside out, and I am having more fun than ever as we expand and grow our business."

At Natori's New York City headquarters, with its white-on-white NATORI sign and orchid-adorned sitting area, every detail of the decor is an expression of Josie's creative vision. She's not merely the head of a fashion business; she is also its heart. Josie is expansive on a range of topics, from the company's current performance to her grandchildren's latest adventures, and her dedication to balancing several commitments at once emerges.

Every month, Josie undertakes an epic journey, traveling seventeen thousand miles round-trip from Natori's corporate home to its manufacturing facility in the Philippines. These business trips include visits with her mother, who even at age one hundred continues to look over the financial health of the Natori Company, which remains family-owned.

The Natori legacy exists at an intersection of art and culture, business and family.

Josie Natori's savvy move from finance to fashion constitutes a master class in the solo creation of dynamic change that defines a **Trailblazer.**

Discerning the Need for a Trailblazer

Trailblazers are especially sensitive to indicators—always powerful, yet often subtle—that signal it's time for a change.

Imagine waking up to a persistent signal. Your intuition acknowledges your many achievements but senses the potential for different experiences.

Perhaps while working your current job or engaged in daily activities, you find yourself frequently lost in thoughts of a life more in tune with your deepest passions. When the endeavors that once sparked joy and excitement in you no longer fuel the fire inside but deplete it, it's a clear sign that a new path awaits.

At night, as the world quiets down, do you find yourself wide-awake, your mind filled with visions that refuse to be ignored? Problems to be solved, or opportunities that have somehow chosen you, whispering relentlessly, "If not you, then who?" An idea that feels uniquely yours, a mission that seems to have been waiting for you to bring it to life. As nights blend into days, this disruptive thought becomes your constant companion, an obsession that won't let you go. It's more than just a fleeting idea—it's a calling. The realization haunts you with the weight and clarity of dawn breaking: making a difference in this specific way, addressing this particular issue, might very well be the path you've been seeking, one that only you can tread.

Whether the change is a subtle ache that grows over time or a sudden shock that stops you in your tracks, it is a powerful catalyst that awakens the positive disrupter in you. These pivotal moments, though daunting, can thrust you into the role of a Trailblazer, one in which you feel compelled to forge a new path not just for survival but also to ignite the fire inside.

Acting as a Trailblazer

Consider Josie, who listened attentively to the call that her Wall Street career was only the beginning of her professional achievements. As she explored avenues where she could make her mark, she discovered a gap in the fashion industry that blended her business aspirations with her Filipina background, a cause close to her heart. It was a calling for her to step up and blaze a trail, to make a difference by honoring her heritage through fashion. This turn of events epitomizes the essence of a Trailblazer: identifying where the fire inside you and the needs of the world intersect and discerning how to best step into that space and make an impact.

Embracing change and venturing out on your own

can occur in many ways. Being a Trailblazer isn't reserved solely for big, bold changes. The work of Trailblazers can show up in minor shifts in daily habits. Yes, some Trailblazers quit their jobs and climb Mount Everest, but the vast majority choose to take smaller steps, such as changing their eating habits, going back to school, starting a side hustle, investing more time and energy into their families, or leading the next project at work. Or maybe you are faced with a sudden and unexpected disruption that has stopped you in your tracks and caused you to realize that the life you are living isn't steering you to the life you envision.

Effective Trailblazers aren't playing a comparison game, caught in a loop of benchmarking themselves against others. They are making moves moment by moment, fueled by the fire inside.

Being a Trailblazer involves asking yourself tough questions as well as seeking guidance and wisdom from those who've navigated similar paths. Whether it's adopting a more healthful lifestyle, initiating a community project, launching a start-up business, changing jobs, or simply choosing to live in a way that feels authentic to you, embracing the role of a Trailblazer means you're not only ready to explore uncharted territory but also prepared to confront any resistance or skepticism that might come your way.

But Keep in Mind...

The journey into the unknown can be both exciting and isolating. There's also the risk of tunnel vision, in which you become so focused on your goals that you ignore new trends or critical feedback. Plus, the burden of carrying all the responsibility for success or failure can be overwhelming and lead to burnout. If you try to go it alone, you might miss out on valuable insights and support, which can lead to overlooking important details or better solutions.

Let's make the concept of a **Trailblazer** real by looking at how it shows up at different levels in an organization.

At the executive level, a senior leader might blaze the trail by leading a research effort to explore a brand-new market that fits the company's future. They are not just managing today's business. They are looking ahead, spotting new opportunities, and helping the organization move toward them.

But trailblazing isn't limited to the executive suite.

In fact, cultures of positive disruption happen when people at every level step up to lead change. A team leader might take on the Trailblazer role by testing a new sales approach with their team. They are willing to try something new, learn from it, and show others a better way forward.

And a team member can be a Trailblazer, too. Maybe they notice a recurring customer problem and take the initiative to fix it. They are not waiting for permission. They see something that needs to change and step up to make it better.

No matter where you are in the organization, Trailblazers are the ones who spot opportunities and take action to move things forward.

TRAILBLAZER

EXECUTIVE	Leads a research effort to explore a new market that fits the company's long-term direction.
TEAM LEADER	Tests a new sales approach to see how it performs before rolling it out with their team.
TEAM MEMBER	Spots a recurring issue and creates and implements a fix that improves a customer problem.

Chapter 11

Firefighter: Seek Stability and Act Independently

Saying no can be an equally courageous path to progress.

Imagine a woman in Latin America or Southeast Asia or Africa who wants to build a business in her community. For all her intelligence, skill, and vision, she lacks access to capital and economic guidance because of the complexities of local financial systems.

Enter Women's World Banking. This global non-profit organization was born out of the first-ever United Nations world conference on the status of women, held during International Women's Year, in 1975.

Ushering in the United Nations Decade for Women (1976–1985), the 1975 conference stated in its final report: "National plans and strategies for the implementation of this Plan should be sensitive to the needs and problems of different categories of women and of women of different age groups. However, Governments should pay special attention to improving the situation of women in areas where they have been most disadvantaged and especially of women in rural and urban areas."

To this end, Women's World Banking addresses low-income women's challenges by partnering with financial institutions, service providers, policymakers, investors, and donors to provide women-centered financial products and services, including financial education, secure payment methods, small-business loans, and basic savings, credit, and insurance plans.

Harsha Rodrigues—executive vice president, regional client services, Southeast Asia, South Asia, Africa, Latin America, and the Caribbean—has been an integral part of Women's World Banking for more than two decades.

Harsha's early life in India shaped her views on cultural expectations and the critical role of financial independence. Encouraged by her family to study abroad, she was drawn by the promise of business travel to join an international management consulting company. However, it wasn't long before she started questioning the real impact of her work.

Harsha's fire inside was dwindling, so when a chat with a former intern introduced her to Women's World Banking, she was intrigued by the organization's mission of self-empowerment for women. Though joining Women's World Banking meant a pay cut and starting over, Harsha was all in, immediately contributing to the organization's growth while helping shift focus from microcredit to a wider mission of financial inclusion.

She has steered the organization through major disruptions, taking on roles that blend pioneering and sustaining progress. At times she has played the roles of both Trailblazer and Torchbearer. Her efforts have helped millions of women around the world gain access to financial services, enabling them to make life choices that fit their individual situations.

At a leadership conference in Massachusetts, Harsha was brought into a conversation around succession, and the opportunity to potentially lead the organization in the future was put forward. An internal leader and mentor whom she continues to remain close to recognized her potential and told her that she had the opportunity to chart her own course as a leader.

"This is a fantastic chance for growth," her mentor said. "Will you consider it?"

Harsha did consider the opportunity, but in the end, she decided to embrace the role of Firefighter.

"When they offered the opportunity to consider the senior leadership role, I turned it down," Harsha says. "I believe leadership can be many things. I'm definitely a leader here; I'm on the executive team, and I have strong opinions. But I prefer to lead from the back. It's about making an impact and finding effective ways to do that, and I've seen it work."

People in Harsha's circle of trust encouraged her to accept the offer. Though she listened attentively to the advice, she knew the best choice was the bold and disruptive one, and she made it.

Discerning the Need for a Firefighter

In the midst of a disruption, a Firefighter understands when to prioritize stability over change and knows that calmness can be an equally courageous path to progress. "To be successful," Harsha says, "one of the most profound leadership principles to live by and remember is that it is not about you."

Recognizing her strengths in strategic oversight, fostering partnerships, and championing financial inclusion from a position that allows her a broad sphere of influence without the constraints of day-to-day leadership duties, she showcased an acute ability to discern the right time to push forward and the right time to hold the line for continuity and stability.

Acting as a Firefighter

If chasing change feels thrilling in the moment, but something in your gut tells you the timing isn't right, it might be time to step up and say no. Maybe your team has already weathered a series of changes, and you're noticing that fatigue from constantly pursuing new opportunities—even exciting ones—is starting to take a toll. Or perhaps you've noticed that chasing the newest fad is pulling you away from what really matters. In that case, doubling down on the path you're already on and leading with conviction might be the right move.

Taking on a Firefighter role can be profoundly disruptive—not because you're charging ahead but because you're choosing to say no to something good, maybe even something great, to focus on what's better.

But Keep in Mind...

Maintaining stability can come with its own set of challenges, including undercommunication, causing others to second-guess your decisions and intentions. The choice to prioritize stability might be seen as mere resistance to change, negatively affecting your reputation and relationships. It's essential to communicate

113

clearly that this strategic choice is about long-term benefits, not an effort to cling to the past or sidestep change.

FIREFIGHTER

EXECUTIVE	Says no to a flashy new tech investment so the company can focus on using what it already has.
TEAM LEADER	Stays committed to the team's main goals, even when there's pressure to chase something new.
TEAM MEMBER	Recommends sticking with the current system instead of switching tools again so the team can stay steady.

Chapter 12

Torchbearer: Seek Change and Act Collaboratively

Go in a different direction and take others with you.

"The day I got kicked out of school," Bill Milliken says, "was the turning point that ultimately led me to a life of service."

When he was a kid, the trouble began with a schoolteacher in Pittsburgh, Pennsylvania, embarrassing him over a reading assignment.

"I struggle with what is called imprinting," Bill explains, a learning challenge that makes it difficult for him to remember what he reads.

Still, he's expelled. After falling in with a rough crowd, he spends his days at a local pool hall, where he makes poor choices and feels hopeless about his future—until a caring adult appears. This man, who volunteered for a youth service organization and spent time working with troubled kids, sets his sights on helping Bill and his friends avoid a life on the streets.

"He spent a year trying to convince some of my friends and me to go a different direction. It's through that experience that I realized that it's relationships that change people, not programs," Bill says.

At age twenty, Bill moves to Harlem with his Pittsburgh pool-hall friend Vinny. It's the 1960s, and in Harlem and the Lower East Side, kids are dropping out of school and living on the streets. Bill has abandoned his middle-class upbringing, and Vinny has turned his back on drug use. Their shared goal is to help kids in the same way they'd been helped by the youth service organization back home.

Communities grappling with poverty, racial tension, and social strife have no safe spaces for troubled youth. So Bill and a network of friends and volunteers persuade a New York City church with substantial property holdings to house kids in empty tenements on the Lower East Side.

But getting kids off the street is only part of the answer. "We realized that we had to do something about education," Bill asserts. They create storefront schools called street academies, and they begin offering General Educational Development (GED) programs and other instructional support.

On July 2, 1964, President Lyndon Johnson signs the Civil Rights Act into law. Two weeks later, a Black teenager is fatally shot in Harlem by an off-duty white police officer. Two days of peaceful protests erupt into six days of violence on the part of eight thousand Harlem residents.

In the aftermath, businesspeople and politicians looking for solutions to social unrest take notice of Bill's work with young people. "If kids don't have hope," Bill advises local leaders, "they'll do one of two things. They're going to hurt you, or they're going to hurt themselves."

In 1977, continuing to believe that educating at-risk students is the best way to support them, Bill founds Communities in Schools (CIS). CIS tackles the nonacademic barriers that prevent students from succeeding. "We need to build a community of resources around the school to free the teachers up to teach and the principals to be principals," Bill says.

Today, CIS operates in more than 3,300 schools in twenty-eight states and the District of Columbia, supporting more than two million students and their families annually. "Love is the only transformational thing we have, and that love is something you do in action," Bill Milliken says. "Love is hope in action!"

From the streets of Harlem to the halls of the United States Congress, Bill has been a persuasive advocate for change. "If you don't look through the eyes of poverty, you're never going to solve the dropout issue," he says, highlighting the importance of understanding the root causes of educational disparities.

"I'm in this for life," says the founder and vice chairman of Communities in Schools.

Discerning the Need for a Torchbearer

A Torchbearer leads a movement to create needed change — and sustain it. A recipient of the Dr. Martin Luther King Jr. Legacy Award, for National Service, as well as the public service community's "Nobel Prize," the Jefferson Award, Bill Milliken holds convictions that are still as strong as the day he moved to New York City determined to help kids like him who risk going down the wrong path but who can be saved by caring communities.

Torchbearers are buoyed by the winds of change, calling for a collective march forward rather than a solitary journey. The motivation to mobilize often springs from a place of personal dissatisfaction or from observing that the familiar no longer serves the greater good.

Bill's sense of urgency was fueled by personal disruptions that started with his own learning struggles and continued as he watched others experiencing challenges related to educational quality and access. Bill is another positive disrupter who redefines possibilities and bridges gaps through collective effort.

Torchbearers echo the traits of Trailblazers, who seek out new directions, but Torchbearers distinguish themselves by rallying others, illuminating the way not only to inspire but also to mobilize collective action.

The decision to lead with and through others in the wake of disruption is sparked by identifying opportunities ripe for joint effort. Such moments arise when the task at hand is too daunting to tackle alone, when diverse perspectives can enrich the solution, or when a vision resonates deeply with the collective aspirations of a community. Embracing the Torchbearer role involves articulating a clear and compelling vision for change — one that serves as a rallying cry for others.

Acting as a Torchbearer

Maybe you're part of a team and something disruptive happens — perhaps a major customer leaves. You assess what could've been done better, whether using resources more wisely or collaborating more effectively. No matter your title, you can take the lead, coordinate the effort, and guide the team to do things differently in the future.

The same applies at home. Perhaps a cherished family member passes away, leaving everyone grieving. You decide to turn this sadness into the beginning of something meaningful—a new family tradition, like an annual reunion that honors their legacy. You can make it happen and bring others with you by lighting the path.

The Torchbearer role, like all of these roles, isn't reserved for someone with a specific title or status. It's open to anyone willing to take it on.

But Keep in Mind...

Mobilizing a group around a shared vision brings its own set of challenges. Managing group dynamics can be tricky, especially when differing opinions start to cloud the original vision. Striving too hard for consensus can lead to indecision and stalled progress. In addition, trying to please everyone can drain your energy and divert focus from the main goals, thus weakening the collective effort. As a Torchbearer, you should be willing to ask honest questions, listen, understand, provide guidance, and make tough decisions.

TORCHBEARER

EXECUTIVE	Pulls together leaders across the company to shape and launch a major new initiative.
TEAM LEADER	Works with different departments to make the customer experience better for everyone.
TEAM MEMBER	Brings coworkers together to fix a client issue that's been slowing everyone down.

Chapter 13

Fire Chief: Seek Stability and Act Collaboratively

Value what came before you in helping others create what comes next.

Picture yourself inside the bustling Bridgestone Arena in the heart of Nashville, Tennessee. The venue is home to the National Hockey League's Nashville Predators and hosts a wide range of sporting events, live shows, and concerts.

Tonight the ice is covered and the air is electric, buzzing with the excitement of nearly fifteen thousand concertgoers who've turned out to see a pair of Nashville residents originally from Belfast, Northern Ireland.

This singing duo isn't Aerosmith, Billie Eilish, Drake, Alan Jackson, Post Malone, or any other entertainer who has rocked Bridgestone in recent years but rather Keith and Kristyn Getty, among the world's most influential modern hymn writers. Backed by a diverse international band of musicians, singers, and dancers, the Gettys and their four young daughters share the spotlight onstage and entertain the crowd.

"It was my parents, John and Helen, who introduced me to my faith," Keith Getty says. "Dad was a choirmaster in the church, and mum was a piano teacher and also introduced me to music."

The flute fascinated young Keith, who at age eighteen traveled to Switzerland to attend a master class with the "man with the golden flute," fellow Belfast native Sir James Galway.

"You are not going to make it as a flute player," Galway told Keith.

The feedback stung initially, but Keith quickly absorbed the disruption. He earned a music degree from England's Durham University and studied conducting in London.

Within months, he was performing with groups and composing and arranging regularly for theater productions, concerts, and British Broadcasting Corporation television and radio programs.

But what emerged was a bigger vision to reinvent the composition of hymns. When Keith began writing new hymns, he set out to create worship music with deep theological roots, challenging what he felt were the oversimplified and less inspiring trends of the time. In doing so, he sparked a movement, demonstrating how a leader can inspire others by staying true to their vision and values.

In his twenties, Keith wrote "piles and piles of melodies," usually on manuscript paper but sometimes on scraps he grabbed when inspiration struck. He had an idea for a hymn about the life of Christ and jotted a basic arrangement on the back of a bill from Northern Ireland Electricity.

I like this, Keith thought, bringing the tune to lyricist Stuart Townend. The result was a hymn in four-verse form they titled "In Christ Alone."

When they first performed the song, Keith says, "the music wasn't finished yet, but the crowd response surprised us." After the final lyric ("Here in the power of Christ I'll stand") nearly three hundred people lined up, humming the melody they had just heard for the first time and requesting copies of the lyrics.

" 'In Christ Alone' was the first hymn that blew the whole thing open for us," Keith says. "I was twenty-five when I wrote it."

That was in 2001. Since then, "In Christ Alone" has been recorded more than two hundred times by a variety of artists and has become a favorite in English-speaking Christian churches worldwide.

The anthem has ushered in a new era of worship music, sparking what is often called the "modern hymn movement," and it continually ranks among the top songs in the Christian Copyright Licensing International (CCLI) charts, which track the most popular workshop songs in churches globally.

"To help articulate the Christian faith and what is behind it" is Keith's goal with every hymn he writes, many of them with Kristyn, including "Christ Our Hope in Life and Death," "Christus Victor," and "The Power of the Cross." Each year, one hundred million churchgoers sing Getty hymns in services. Among the five hundred most frequently sung hymns in the United States and the UK, thirty-eight of them have Getty Music copyrights.

Fast-forward a few months from the big stage at Bridgestone Arena, and Keith is seated across a table, describing a work-life balance that includes "writing hymns and raising 'hers'"—his and Kristyn's four daughters, who go to school in Nashville and benefit from the education travel provides. "If we are in New York, they will tour around Manhattan," Keith says. "If we are in Washington, DC, they will visit two museums a day, and in Ireland they get to explore."

International travel is part of Getty family life, though they limit touring to twelve weeks a year. Keith and Kristyn perform annually to sold-out crowds at Carnegie

125

Hall, the Kennedy Center, the Sydney Opera House, Royal Albert Hall, and the Grand Ole Opry.

In 2018, Keith and Kristyn are invited guests of Queen Elizabeth II at Holyrood Palace, in Edinburgh, Scotland, where the monarch presents Keith with the gilded silver badge commemorating his new status as Officer of the Order of the British Empire, the first contemporary church musician to be so recognized.

"When I first received the call, I was pretty surprised," Keith says. "It is an honor for us as a family and also for the great hymn-writing heritage we have here in the UK of which we are a tiny part."

Blending deep theology, great artistry, and community building through concerts and resources, the global footprint of Getty Music continues to grow, breathing new life into a historic art form. In 2020, the Getty Music Foundation was established as an educational mission to preserve and revitalize congregational singing in areas with limited resources. The annual Sing! conference draws thousands—more than 6,500 in 2024—to the Opryland convention center, in Nashville, to sing hymns while a live-streamed audience of more than thirty thousand tunes in.

A concert organizer who's traveled from Wales to volunteer says, "I want people to come and hear the

Bible and be ministered to. The Gettys' goal is to teach the Scriptures, evangelize the world, and reach whole families."

The audience is multigenerational and international, representing all fifty states and more than thirty countries.

On a family trip to Sing!, a grandfather who's brought along his daughter and grandchildren says, "The Gettys don't mince words about what Christ did for us. The music is theologically rich."

Keith explains the depths of his calling: "I believe singing transforms people, and getting individuals, families and children singing again is our life's work."

Being a Fire Chief is not simply about seeking stability to avoid innovation and creativity. Keith Getty's work is all about innovation and creativity. He shows how as the leader of a movement, you can use innovation and creativity to move others back to something deeper and richer—something timely yet timeless. Keith is a Fire Chief, moving away from the prevailing trends and preserving what he values in past traditions.

Discerning the Need for a Fire Chief

Embracing the role of a Fire Chief often starts with asking key questions of your family, team, or organization: Why do we exist? What is our purpose? What drives us at our core? And how can we stay true to that purpose, even in the face of disruption?

When you're thinking about whether to step into the role of a Fire Chief, be it as the leader of an organization or a community or social movement, there are several things to consider.

Start by looking at how often and in what ways disruptions are affecting your team, organization, industry, relationships, or family. If you find that these challenges continually throw things off track and distract from your main goals or a deeper purpose, it could be a clear signal that a steadier hand on the wheel is needed. This is especially true if these disruptions are more than minor bumps in the road.

It's also smart to tune in to the feedback you're receiving from those around you. If there's a sense of uncertainty or if people feel they're lacking direction, this often points to a need for greater stability or a return to something deeper. People generally look for someone who can clear up confusion and bring a sense of security, especially during uncertain times.

Another important factor is how cohesive your vision is. If you notice that your strategic direction keeps shifting or if there's a misalignment around your long-term goals, stepping in as a Fire Chief can help bring everyone back to focus and ensure that efforts aren't wasted on frequent changes in direction.

Acting as a Fire Chief

Take a moment to consider the costs associated with repeatedly chasing new opportunities. If you're finding that this chase is more costly than beneficial, it might be time to consider strengthening what you already have rather than looking for the next big thing.

Don't overlook external factors such as market volatility, industry disruptions, and even broad societal changes. These can also suggest a need for a leader who buffers unpredictable external forces. Finally, reflect on your readiness and capabilities. Do you feel equipped with the foresight, influence, and collaborative skills needed to lead a movement toward stability? Being self-aware and confident in your abilities is crucial; these traits are as important as any external show of assertiveness.

Becoming a Fire Chief involves a careful blend of understanding both the environment around you and your strengths and readiness to lead. When these elements align, and you feel prepared to guide with strength and insight, stepping into the Fire Chief role can be a game changer for your team at work or your family at home.

But Keep in Mind...

Balancing innovation with tradition requires careful communication in order to harmonize various perspectives and efforts among the team. While achieving consensus is important, it can slow down decision-making during crises. A balance between democratic leadership and decisive action is necessary. Moreover, avoiding bureaucratic delays is essential—too many approval layers can hinder swift action. Streamlining processes while involving key stakeholders effectively is crucial to maintaining momentum.

FIRE CHIEF

EXECUTIVE	Brings the company back to its core values and long-term goals while others chase quick wins.
TEAM LEADER	Creates a simple plan to keep people focused on what's important during a company-wide shift.
TEAM MEMBER	Starts weekly check-ins to help the team stay on track during a time of change.

Chapter 14

Tinder Gatherer: Pursue Clarity and Provide Support

Equip yourself and others to make smart choices.

Attorney Robert Barnett is continually on the phone or in meetings.

His clients range from bestselling authors needing advice about pending book deals to on-screen personalities looking to lock in their contracts with TV networks. But he also has a fascinating expertise: debate preparation for US presidential hopefuls.

Robert's experience in presidential campaigns is unparalleled. He doesn't just prepare candidates for these high-stakes events; he also becomes their strategic ally, diving deep into the opposition's mindset and crafting responses that will resonate with the entire nation. He does so with the intensity and focus that can turn the tide of an election.

He's worked on the ten national campaigns between 1976 and 2012, focusing primarily on debate preparation. In 1984, he takes on the role of George H. W. Bush in practice sessions with Geraldine Ferraro and again in 1988 with Michael Dukakis. While sparring with Bill Clinton during the 1992 campaign, Robert plays the opposition in more than twenty mock debates.

Fast-forward to 2000, and Robert steps into Dick Cheney's shoes to help Joe Lieberman prepare, a role he continues in 2004 to assist John Edwards. In 2000 and 2006, Robert helps Hillary Rodham Clinton with her Senate debate preparations and is instrumental in prepping her for presidential primary debates in 2008. Barack Obama seeks Robert's expertise for debate negotiation and preparation in both 2008 and 2012.

Before the 2016 debates, Robert again plays the role of Bernie Sanders during primary rehearsals with Secretary Clinton and the role of Mike Pence to help prepare Tim Kaine for the vice-presidential debates.

From his roots in Waukegan, Illinois, to his status as a cornerstone of Washington's whirlwind politics and media, Robert's story is nothing short of remarkable. With a sharp mind honed at the University of Wisconsin and the University of Chicago Law School, followed by critical learning under Judge John Minor

Wisdom and Justice Byron White, Robert was clearly going places. But it's not just his brainpower that got him there; it's also his particular approach to disruptions — big and small.

Robert does some of his best work — fueling the fire inside himself and others — when he helps people make decisions and take action with strategy and insight. When his clients are faced with disruption, he's the guy who supports their efforts through advice, counsel, and intelligence gathering. Similarly, in the literary and media worlds, when bestselling authors and TV personalities hit a "difficult situation," they dial Robert's number. Whether it's crisis management, a tricky contract negotiation, or just sage advice, he's the one they want on their side.

His story isn't just one of high-profile names and critical moments in politics and culture — although there are plenty of those. It's also a story about how intellectual agility and a deep commitment to serving others can shape the world from behind the scenes. It speaks volumes about the power of engaging with disruption in thoughtful, productive ways.

Robert knows when to push forward with a strategy, when to pull back and collect more information, and when to stand beside his clients, offering the support they need to navigate their challenges. It's this balance of action and reflection, of leading and supporting, that makes him so effective as a Tinder Gatherer.

Whether he's on that mock debate stage or answering a call for advice, Robert Barnett is living proof that being a Tinder Gatherer isn't about making just any move; it's about making the smart move.

Discerning the Need for a Tinder Gatherer

Adopting the role of a Tinder Gatherer is particularly crucial in environments where change is not immediately necessary or might even be counterproductive. Robert Barnett's work, especially in preparing political figures for debates, showcases the importance of creating a secure, well-prepared foundation amid the constant flux of the political landscape.

This role becomes pertinent when the situation calls for a temporary pause, allowing for a period of assessment, information gathering, and collective decision-making. Recognizing when to step into this role, much like Robert's strategic approach to navigating the political and legal spheres, involves a nuanced understanding of the current climate and the needs of those around you.

Tinder Gatherers often arise when the atmosphere is saturated with change to the point where additional turmoil could lead to instability or diminish people's capacity to adapt effectively. In such moments, the collective benefit lies in fostering a stable environment, one that supports growth and development at a sustainable pace.

Acting as a Tinder Gatherer

When faced with uncertainty, or a future fraught with too many unknowns, acting as a Tinder Gatherer helps you and others focus on consolidating current strengths and resources. This approach allows for a measured evaluation of the situation, ensuring that any future changes are well-informed and mutually agreed upon. The Tinder Gatherer role often provides the calm, strategic insight necessary to navigate uncertain times, dispensing critical advice that helps people leverage their strengths and resources.

The need for this role is also evident when there's a collective sense of readiness for change but the timing isn't right. Perhaps external factors necessitate a period of waiting, or the group needs more time to gather vital information and achieve consensus. In these instances, a Tinder Gatherer helps anchor the group, providing a calm, reflective space in which everyone can understand the implications of their choices fully.

Robert's decision-making process, informed by years of experience and a deep understanding of the broad implications of political actions, highlights this aspect of being a measured and insightful partner.

If you perceive that rapid changes have left your team, relationships, or family feeling unmoored, taking the time to slow things down can be a powerful way to reground and realign. By advocating for a pause, you allow everyone to catch their collective breath, reassess the direction they are moving in, and decide how to create a sense of purpose, clarity, and commitment.

But Keep in Mind....

Focusing too much on gathering information can lead to analysis paralysis, delaying necessary actions. It's important to ensure that the insights you gather are effectively integrated into decision-making processes. In addition, the Tinder Gatherer's role might be undervalued, so advocate for the resources and recognition you need to perform the role. Smart Tinder Gatherers are great communicators who ensure that their intentions are conveyed and their contributions understood. Failing to do so may cause others to make assumptions that miss the mark.

TINDER GATHERER

EXECUTIVE	Brings forward outside perspectives that help leadership think ahead and make better decisions.
TEAM LEADER	Shares key customer feedback to help shape a new idea the team is working on.
TEAM MEMBER	Pulls together research and trends that help the team prepare for what's ahead.

Quick Recap: Discern

In navigating life's disruptions, you can take on one of five distinct **Positive Disrupter Roles**.

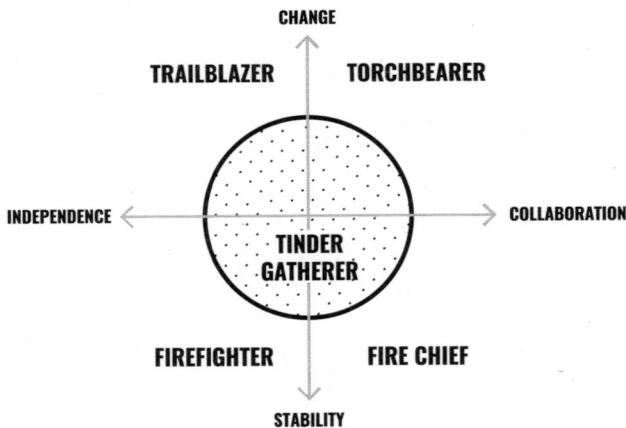

- **Trailblazer:** Seek Change and Act Independently — This role is for innovators who challenge the status quo independently in order to bring about progress and new ideas.

- **Firefighter:** Seek Stability and Act Independently — This role is for people who are adept at working independently to end undue or rapid shifts that could destabilize or water down their effectiveness.
- **Torchbearer:** Seek Change and Act Collaboratively — This role is for leaders who rally others toward shared goals and capitalize on the momentum of change.
- **Fire Chief:** Seek Stability and Act Collectively — This role is for leaders who see change as a distraction from something more important and work with and through others to create a movement that focuses on what truly matters most.
- **Tinder Gatherer:** Pursue Clarity and Provide Support — This role is for collaborators focused on information gathering and teamwork, ensuring that decisions are timely, that information is available, and that those around them are well supported.

Discernment involves understanding your ambitions, grasping the realities of your current situation, and honoring your relationships.

It is essential to choose the right role at the right

time based on a comprehensive understanding of yourself and your environment.

Crafting your good life is about intentional action and the wise discernment of when and how to act, ensuring that each decision aligns with your path to fulfillment.

In pursuit of your good life, you will play each of these roles at various times, depending on the disruptions you face.

Disrupting Beyond Yourself

Here's a disruptive idea: What if these roles aren't just for individuals? What if you work together with others to take on a role as a group? Suddenly, the question about individual versus collective becomes: Should my team, group, or family take this on by ourselves or with other teams, groups, and families? Should we work together for stability or change?

Your family might decide to be a Trailblazing family, packing up and moving to a new town or taking on an adventure that helps everyone grow together. Your customer service team could step into the Fire Chief role, doubling down on the basics of great customer care and reigniting their passion for serving others. Or maybe your community takes on the Torchbearer role, rallying other groups to help build a park — a space that brings people together and leaves a lasting legacy.

If you and those around you can consciously take on the right role at the right time, you can make a huge impact.

Moving from Role to Role

Emma leads a product support team at a growing tech company. For months, she'd been noticing a trend — support tickets for one feature were increasing, but customer satisfaction around that same feature was dropping.

At first, Emma played the **Tinder Gatherer** role.

She didn't rush to make noise. Instead, she quietly gathered data — customer feedback, ticket resolution times, internal system logs. She listened closely in team meetings and asked thoughtful questions in cross-functional check-ins. She wanted to be sure before pushing for change. When the picture became clear, she didn't wait for someone else to act.

That's when she stepped into the **Trailblazer** role.

Emma took the initiative to draft a short report and proposed a focused fix. She didn't just suggest it — she tested it with her team on a few key cases, saw immediate improvement, and shared the early success with her manager. Her idea got attention not because it was loud, but because it worked.

As momentum built, Emma became a **Torchbearer.**

With early results in hand, she reached out to peer team leaders and product managers, inviting them to help scale the solution. She hosted a short session to walk through the fix, shared tools and templates her team had created, and encouraged others to tailor it for their own workflows. What started as insight turned into action—then into a shared movement for better customer outcomes.

MOVING FROM ROLE TO ROLE

As Emma moves from one role to another, she recognizes that as the situation changes and new opportunities emerge, she too can change her contribution. This is a critical idea. None of us are fixed in a certain role. It's a choice.

TINDER GATHERER	Instead of reacting immediately, she gathers data (customer feedback, internal metrics, and team insights) to fully understand the problem.
TRAILBLAZER	Once clear, Emma tests a small fix with her team, proves it works, and shares the results with leadership to spark interest.
TORCHBEARER	With momentum behind her, she brings in other team leads, shares tools and lessons learned, and helps scale the solution across departments.

Part IV
Behave

Chapter 15

The Anatomy of a Positive Disrupter

Mindset is essential, but behaviors deliver results.

There's a special pressure that comes with being chosen first. In childhood, you might feel it when you're called on in class, when you're chosen as team captain in a playground game, or when you're cast as the lead in the school play. But almost no pressure is greater than if you're the top pick in the Major League Baseball (MLB) draft.

Chicago Cubs shortstop Dansby Swanson knows all about delivering under this type of pressure. As the number one pick in the 2015 draft, Dansby made the journey from an under-the-radar high school athlete to an MLB All-Star, a testament to his talent, relentless effort, preparation, and commitment.

"There are certain things you have to do consistently,

whether it's your training, skills, or mental preparation," Dansby says. He understands that while dreams, talents, and grand plans are important, delivering on them requires consistently adopting the right behaviors. You must take action to make a difference.

Despite significant setbacks, including injuries and unexpected trades, his commitment and work ethic propel him to become a 2021 World Series champion with the Atlanta Braves, a two-time Gold Glove winner, and an MLB All-Star in 2022 and 2023.

Dansby emphasizes the importance of daily habits and routines. For example, his day always includes early morning Scripture reading, physical training, and exercises that keep him focused and resilient.

Dansby's disciplined approach is crucial to his success. He meticulously plans his days, ensuring that every activity is geared toward optimal performance. Whether he is dealing with an injury or any other kind of setback, he understands that embracing the right behaviors is key to moving forward. These behaviors allow him to improve, deliver results, and focus his energy in the right places. He can't control who's on the mound for the opposing team or if a defensive player makes a once-in-a-lifetime catch, but he can control his own approach when stepping into the batter's box or taking his position at shortstop.

"Failure happens so often in our game. The more

you can compartmentalize it and move forward, the better off you'll be," Dansby says. He knows that striking out and dropping the ball are part of playing the game. He isn't afraid of messing up. He just wants the bat in his hands.

"Winning starts with the mentality," Dansby says. "It starts with the belief, each and every day, that you're not showing up *wanting* to win, you're showing up that you're *going* to win. It's never a matter of 'if.' It's just a matter of 'when.'"

For anyone ready to step up to the plate in their own lives, remember that dreaming is just the start. It's the actions you take, the routines you build, and the behaviors you develop that will ultimately lead you to success.

As you move from discernment to behavior, realize that no matter which disruptive role you play (Trailblazer, Firefighter, Torchbearer, Fire Chief, or Tinder Gatherer), each has inherent challenges that will demand your best efforts.

The Behaviors of a Positive Disrupter

Being a positive disrupter isn't about having one standout quality. Success is found in a combination of behaviors, each making an important contribution. Consider the **Anatomy of a Positive Disrupter** as a way of organizing behaviors into pairs, and assigning each pair to a body part. Think of it as taking a head-to-toe inventory of yourself. It's based on the sixteen behaviors we saw over and over as we interviewed hundreds of positive disrupters.

Do you need to excel in all of these behaviors to be successful? Absolutely not.

Positive disrupters, like all of us, have strengths and weaknesses. Dansby Swanson, for example. As an outstanding baseball player, he has both positive points and areas needing improvement. But he's surrounded by teammates whose strengths compensate for his weaknesses. You should do the same. Seek insight and counsel from others and continue to learn and grow. These actions are critical to achieving success. Remember, like baseball, life is a relationship game and a team sport.

Now let's take a look at the behavior pairs.

Brain

Behavior 1: Think Deeply to Uncover Insights

Engage your brain in continual curiosity, seeking the wisdom that lies beneath the surface.

Behavior 2: Believe Better Is Possible

Harness your brain's optimism, believing in the potential for improvement in every situation.

Eyes

Behavior 3: Have a Vision

Use your eyes to look ahead, imagining possibilities that others haven't yet seen.

Behavior 4: See Brutal Reality

Acknowledge the hard truths of the present without flinching from the challenges.

Ears

Behavior 5: Listen to Understand

Truly listen, ask good questions, capture the full essence of conversations, and understand others' points of view.

Behavior 6: Hear What's Not Said

Tune in to the silence, picking up on unsaid messages that can be just as powerful as those articulated.

Mouth

Behavior 7: Say Something Smart

Speak with intention, offering insights that provoke thought and action.

Behavior 8: Stay on Message

Keep your communication consistent, reinforcing your core message across all platforms.

Heart

Behavior 9: Care About Others

Show empathy, driving changes that resonate on a deeply personal level.

Behavior 10: Act on Your Conscience

Align your actions with your values, choosing the right path over the easy one.

Gut

Behavior 11: Trust Your Instincts

Listen to your inner voice and let it guide you through the unknown with confidence.

Behavior 12: Push Past the Butterflies

Embrace nerves as a sign of impending growth and leap forward with courage.

Hands

Behavior 13: Let Go of Good to Get Better

Be ready to release the present to grasp a more promising future.

Behavior 14: Get Your Hands Dirty

Engage in the hard work necessary to bring your vision to life.

Feet

Behavior 15: Run Toward Disruption

Be proactive in facing change, leading the charge into new territories.

Behavior 16: Stand Firm Despite Doubters

Remain steadfast in your beliefs, even in the face of skepticism.

Read on to further explore all sixteen behaviors of a positive disrupter, and how to put them into practice in your daily life.

~~~~~~~~~~~~~~~~~~~~~~~~~~~~~~~~~~

Positive Disuptor Move

Name Your Greatness

Take 60 seconds today to name the behaviors you're great at. List them. Own them. Use one with intention today.

Want to assess your own behaviors and those of your team? Check out "Tool 7: Assess Your 16 Key Behaviors" in Part VII. You can fill out the worksheet as you learn about the behaviors in the subsequent chapters.

~~~~~~~~~~~~~~~~~~~~~~~~~~~~~~~~~~

Chapter 16
Brain

Envision what others fail to see.

"We make generic gummy bears," the client says, "and we often end up with scrap...transitioned colors, misshapen bears, you name it. We could ship it off to a pig farmer for feed, but can you help us figure out how to make better use of it?"

This might not be a typical request for most businesses, but for David Mendelson, it's just another day at the office. His company thrives on transforming daily disruptions into viable opportunities.

David and his team view by-products not as waste but as valuable assets. Their mission is to create innovative ways to repurpose these discarded items, transforming them into both environmentally friendly *and* profitable ventures. As he explains, "Our business deals with industrial by-products. Raw materials coming into a manufacturing facility don't always match the finished goods leaving it, creating friction points where by-products are generated. This could be as simple as a corrugated box from a distribution center or as complex as by-products from manufacturing artificial skin for burn victims."

When faced with the gummy bear scrap problem, David and his team came up with a creative solution: They located another client who was struggling to improve the bait used to lure grizzly bears away from residential areas. While the bears had grown indifferent to traditional bait over time, the gummy bear scrap proved (ironically!) irresistible. David's team connected the gummy bear company with the bear-bait manufacturer and produced a triple benefit: The bait manufacturer found a better raw material, the bears were safely captured, and the gummy bear company had a more valuable—and dependable—market for its by-products.

"We do not only create revenue, but eliminate costs too. Whether it is the sale of a newly identified by-product, the elimination of landfill costs or the streamlining of material handling within the process, all of our work falls to the bottom line of our clients," David says.

David is the latest link in a one-hundred-year-long

chain of creative thinking and innovation. His journey is deeply rooted in his family's entrepreneurial spirit, beginning with his great-grandfather, an immigrant who came to America without a dollar to his name and without speaking a word of English, and helped revolutionize the scrap industry.

In the early 1900s, David's great-grandfather and his sons established Waterway Paper Products in Chicago, the first paper mill in the United States to use 100 percent recycled newspapers rather than wood chips to make new newsprint. The mill produced all the newsprint for the *Chicago Daily News* and created a market for the by-product of the mass production of information: newspapers. Unfortunately, when this innovation caught the eye of a big player in the paper industry, the family was pressured into selling the mill— and then lost the proceeds in the stock market crash of 1929. Despite this setback, the Mendelson family's spirit of innovation remained unbroken.

David's father, Robert, later founded Donco Paper Supply Company, and now under David's leadership, Donco comprises several entities—Donco Paper itself, along with Ohio Pulp Mills, Poly Recyclers, and Ramblin Corp—all of which focus on making recycling economically viable.

Whether it's using by-products from clothing manufacturing to solve problems in the coffin-making

154

business or transforming scrap from diaper production into fake snow for theatrical performances, Donco exemplifies the behaviors of thinking deeply and believing that better is possible. In small regional firms as well as international businesses, opportunities present themselves when scrap is looked at through a creative lens.

This approach has cultivated a team dedicated to intriguing, intellectually stimulating work — including David's ninety-year-old father, who continues to contribute to the team's deep thinking and innovative solutions.

"As proud as I am of our family business, I am much prouder of our business family," David says. At the heart of Donco's achievements is a culture that values relationships, family, innovation, and a collective commitment to making a difference.

This ethos is celebrated through traditions such as the Donco Threshold, which celebrates the many team members who spend more than half their lives working with the company and those who transition to emeritus status rather than retire, preserving the firm's legacy of knowledge and experience. "No one ever retires from Donco," David states, highlighting the sense of belonging and dedication that defines the company's culture.

David Mendelson's story demonstrates a long-term

commitment to innovation, driven by the belief that through deep thinking, every challenge presents an opportunity for improvement and positive disruption. It is also a wonderful example of the first two positive disrupter behaviors.

Behavior 1: Think Deeply to Uncover Insights

It takes effort and ingenuity to uncover true insights, which are distinguished by their value and originality.

For David and his colleagues, each project presents an opportunity to reimagine recycling's possibilities. This approach has led to pioneering solutions that go beyond mere waste management and create sustainable, economically viable products. "We look at our business kind of like a giant jigsaw puzzle, but sometimes, the pieces that we put together come from different puzzle boxes," David explains, underscoring the creativity and analytical thought involved in their work.

Behavior 2: Believe Better Is Possible

Amid the ever-changing dynamics of the recycling industry, David's optimism anchors Donco. Inspired by his family's history of resilience, he sees every challenge as a stepping stone toward a greener future.

"Recycling is economics," he asserts, emphasizing the idea of achieving sustainability goals and reducing his company's environmental footprint through economically sound practices. He and his team don't just focus on whether a by-product can be put to good use; they also focus on profitability, asking how clients can reuse it in a way that makes financial sense and is economically sustainable.

Reflect on Your Behaviors

Have you looked beneath the surface to find innovative solutions to problems? Reflect on these moments and appreciate the power of deep thinking.

Recall a time when a positive outlook helped you overcome a challenge. How did optimism transform the situation?

Quick Challenge

Consider the challenges and disruptions in your life or work. How can you apply a Mendelson-like approach — combining deep thinking with a belief that better is possible — to transform these challenges into opportunities for growth? Observe how adopting this mindset can lead to innovative solutions that positively affect both your personal life and professional life.

JAMES PATTERSON

Positive Disrupter Move

Applaud Someone Crushing It

Notice what someone's doing right and say it. Out loud.

Chapter 17

Eyes

Collaboration raises creativity to a higher power.

"You have to keep reinventing yourself," Joel Anderson says.

It may sound like a bit of a cliché, yet Joel is anything but. His life is a testament to having a vision and dealing with reality.

Joel Anderson's design career is born from a passion for creating unforgettable album covers. Long before the invention of MP3s and digital streaming, music fans cherish the art and design on vinyl record-album sleeves and CD covers almost as much as the music itself. In 1993, Joel and his business partner launch a design studio in the heart of Music City—Nashville, Tennessee. In an era when music and art are inseparable, their design studio flourishes.

By 2007, however, Joel faces a harsh reality. The industry that had once been fertile creative ground is shifting. When his partner takes early retirement, Joel retools. He has to confront these changes head-on while clinging to the vision he has for his work and for the creative design studio he's always dreamed of building.

Fortunately, Joel's adaptability leads him to a new venture: national parks posters with a timeless, romantic feel. He realizes the potential of this new direction when a calendar of his travel poster art receives acclaim. *Maybe we're onto something,* he thinks. Though he's not on the path he planned, the calendar's style and design give him a new way to achieve his grand vision.

Anderson Design Group's creations now specialize in vintage-style travel posters inspired by the golden age of poster art. Joel's process is hands-on, starting whenever possible with visiting and photographing the destinations in person. After returning from an adventure, he and his artists begin an intricate process of reviewing the reference photos and sketching, then moving on to drawing, painting, and hand-lettering before finally refining the work digitally.

This dedication to classic craftsmanship allows Joel and his team to create more than three thousand illustrated designs, including a series of posters for each national park. Joel's commitment to high-quality

American-made nostalgic travel decor earns his company global success and recognition.

The day before his fifty-fifth birthday, Joel is diagnosed with Parkinson's disease.

Instead of allowing the disruptive diagnosis to end his creative pursuits, though, Joel chooses to view it as an opportunity rather than a limitation. Though it's harder to use his hands, he says, "that's all the more reason to collaborate with other creative people. Also, one of the few ways to slow the progression of Parkinson's disease is to engage in regular, vigorous exercise—like hiking. And the best places to hike in America happen to be in the national parks! While my fine motor skills for drawing, painting, or writing are deteriorating rapidly, I still have a five-to-ten-year window to continue hiking and traveling."

Today, Joel Anderson sees his role as less of a hands-on artist and more of a "conductor," orchestrating the talents of a diverse team to realize his artistic vision. He's dedicated himself to teaching others the craft, relying on them to produce new designs under his direction. This collaborative spirit not only compensates for the loss of his fine motor skills but also enriches his work. "When I collaborate with other artists, we can create things that none of us could do by ourselves," Joel explains.

Since his Parkinson's diagnosis, Joel has also built strategic partnerships to expand the distribution of the growing number of designs his team is creating. Their artwork is now available on various licensed products, including decorative accents for the home, journals, art prints, postcards, puzzles, board games, apparel, and much more.

Joel's response to his diagnosis demonstrates a deep understanding of the reality he faces paired with an optimistic outlook that drives him to adapt and innovate. Despite the challenges posed by Parkinson's, his vision remains clear: to produce creative work that thrills clients and inspires people. While a hands-on approach may no longer be possible, his spirit of collaboration ensures that his creative legacy continues to thrive.

Joel's story showcases the essence of two crucial aspects of the Anatomy of a Positive Disrupter: having a vision and looking closely at the brutal reality of a situation. Through Anderson Design Group, he has navigated the ups and downs of industry trends and personal challenges with a forward-thinking approach and a grounded perspective.

Joel Anderson's story is not just an example of personal triumph but also a powerful example of positive disrupter behaviors 3 and 4.

Behavior 3: Have a Vision

Joel Anderson's ability to have a vision is evident in Anderson Design Group's story. He works to transcend the ordinary, using poster art to celebrate travel, adventure, and the beauty of America's national parks. This isn't just about adapting to change but also about foreseeing a future in which art connects people to their cherished memories and dreams. Joel sees the potential for art as more than just a visual experience: It can become a conversation piece, evoking emotion, nostalgia, and a sense of connection among adventure lovers.

Behavior 4: See Brutal Reality

Facing the brutal reality of changes in his business and, later, his Parkinson's diagnosis, Joel doesn't retreat but instead embraces these challenges with courage and pragmatism. When he sees declines in advertising and design work, he realizes he needs to "come up with new ways to keep using our talents." So he pivots to travel poster art, calendars, and eventually national park posters. His forward-looking approach not only salvages his business, it redefines it, creating a beloved brand that resonates with adventurers and dreamers alike.

Acknowledging the progressive nature of his Parkinson's diagnosis, Joel Anderson adapts his artistic process, focusing on collaboration and direction over manual creation. This is about more than finding a workaround; it's a profound acceptance of reality paired with an undimmed passion for his craft. Through this acceptance, Joel not only continues to contribute to the art world but testifies to the resilience of the human spirit in the face of adversity.

This blend of visionary thinking and a grounded acknowledgment of reality underscores Joel's journey, offering a blueprint for navigating life's inevitable disruptions.

Reflect on Your Behaviors

Joel Anderson's story speaks to the strength found in facing reality head-on while holding fast to a vision for the future. Consider the following questions:

How do you balance your aspirations with the realities of the difficulties and constraints you face?

In what ways can collaboration amplify your ability to overcome challenges and achieve your goals?

Quick Challenge

Identify an area in your life or work where you face obstacles. Apply Joel's approach by envisioning a bold future and meticulously assessing your current situation. Consider who can join you in transforming this vision into reality through collaboration and shared expertise.

Positive Disrupter Move

Ask a Better Question

Move past "How are you?" and spark a real conversation.

Chapter 18

Ears

Find the best team members. Then create positions around them.

Vanessa Ogle knows how to pivot.

She starts her first company, Enseo (pronounced "en-*say*-oh"; Latin for "to think and to do"), in 2000, mainly selling technology to financial services companies such as Reuters and Bloomberg. Things go well—so well that within a year, Vanessa has turned it into an $8 million business.

And then 9/11 occurs. "Our primary business was the financial services industry—ugh—and travel business—ouch," she recalls. She keeps shifting her business model and by 2012 has found a new niche: in-room entertainment. "It didn't matter whether they were cruise ships, big hotels, small hotels, fancy hotels, cheap hotels, we were the technology backbone provider for all of those big boys in the space," Vanessa says.

Enseo is the realization of Vanessa's bold vision to shake up the hospitality industry through cutting-edge in-room entertainment and technology solutions.

Starting from scratch, Enseo grows to be a key player in the business, serving more than eighty-five million guests annually in hotels worldwide at thousands of hotel properties, including Marriotts, Hiltons, and InterContinentals. The secret to its success? Relentless innovation. Enseo racks up 130 US patents (with Vanessa as lead inventor on at least forty of them) and pours more than $80 million into research and development, forging exclusive partnerships with big names such as Netflix and expanding into streaming services with Amazon, HBO, and Hulu.

Then in March of 2020, the entire world is rocked by the COVID-19 pandemic, leaving almost no country or industry unscathed.

The hospitality business is hit especially hard as global hotel occupancy rates plummet. Eight out of ten hotel rooms sit empty in the United States, and the industry is financially hemorrhaging as revenue declines quickly approach 50 percent and hotel-employee layoffs near 70 percent.

This disruption devastates Vanessa Ogle and her team at Enseo, gutting their core market.

Determined to save her company—and the people whose livelihoods depend on it—Vanessa goes into brainstorming mode. "Vanessa comes up with ideas and will bounce them off of us. They'll either go somewhere or they won't," says Enseo's director of engineering. "Brainstorming, coming up with ideas, is right in her wheelhouse. This just kicked her up a notch in what she does best." As one of her top hotel clients puts it, "Vanessa is a class-act person, great business lady, mother and mentor. She sees the future. She's adjusting to what the consumer and the industry demand."

Vanessa's leadership style is the beating heart of Enseo's growth, and her company culture is based on communication, trust, and engagement. It is one in which every voice is valued and innovation is encouraged to be fearless. She believes that listening—to customers, employees, and the market—is just as crucial as technology. This culture of attentive listening and openness to change set Enseo up to tackle unparalleled disruption.

This sensitivity leads to actions such as securing hardship grants for furloughed employees and renegotiating contracts with struggling hotel partners. Vanessa's initiative spurs Enseo to develop and deploy products such as VERA, a remote check-in agent that reduces the need for face-to-face interactions, and CleanLight, a portable UV-C disinfection cart, as a direct response to unvoiced needs. Soon they become staples in the industry. When COVID-19 turned the world upside down, Vanessa relied on two behaviors that are key to the success of many positive disrupters.

Behavior 5: Listen to Understand

Vanessa doesn't just hold meetings to give out information; she also listens closely to her executive team's analyses, concerns, and ideas. She reaches out to clients for business talks and to understand their fears, challenges, and needs during a global crisis. This deep listening informs Enseo's decisions, from implementing employee safety measures to developing products that meet the moment's needs.

Behavior 6: Hear What's Not Said

Vanessa has a knack for picking up on the unspoken worries and needs of others, and she relies on this skill when navigating difficult situations. She recognizes her employees' and customers' anxieties and uncertainties even when they can't voice them themselves.

Vanessa Ogle shows that the essence of leadership in times of disruption isn't about how loudly you speak but how attentively you listen. By truly understanding what isn't said, Vanessa leads Enseo through one of the toughest periods in the company's history. Her leadership guides her company through the crisis while strengthening the trust and loyalty of her team and clients, and laying a solid foundation for resilience and continued innovation in the face of uncertainty.

Reflect on Your Behaviors

Have you ever encountered a situation in which listening closely allowed you to better understand a person or set of circumstances? How did this deeper understanding influence your response and reveal insights about empathy and connection?

Can you recall a time when you sensed something important that wasn't directly communicated? How did recognizing the silent signals lead you to act in a way that had a meaningful impact?

Quick Challenge

Inspired by Vanessa Ogle's use of deep listening and attunement to the unspoken, identify an area in your life or work that could benefit from these approaches. Commit to one actionable step that applies these principles. Perhaps consider addressing an unvoiced need in your community, offering support when it's not explicitly asked for, or simply being present for someone in silence. Embrace this as an opportunity to foster connection, understanding, and positive change, drawing from your innermost values and the power of attentive listening.

Positive Disrupter Move

Finish the Thing

You know the one. Don't overthink, just knock it out.

Chapter 19
Mouth

Speak with intention and consistency.

Picture yourself in your early twenties, fresh-faced and stepping into the vibrant world of New York sportswriting. That's where Mike Lupica found himself, launching a career that would eventually make him a household name. He laughs as he talks about his early days.

"There was a Super Bowl dinner with some older sportswriters — including Red Smith — and my sports editor at the time," Mike says. "And there was a conversation about who the next great sports columnist might be. The next Red, basically. When the dinner was over, my editor said Red, one of my heroes, whispered to him, 'You might not have to look far.' I never thought of myself as being in Red's class and still don't.

But in a world before anybody spoke of street cred, one of the greatest columnists who ever lived had given some to me."

Red Smith truly was a sportswriting legend. Born Walter Wellesley Smith on September 25, 1905, he became renowned for his wit, elegance, and insightful commentary on sports. Starting his journalism career in the 1920s, he wrote for newspapers such as the *Milwaukee Sentinel,* the *St. Louis Star-Times,* and the *New York Herald Tribune* before becoming a columnist for the *New York Times.* His work earned him a Pulitzer Prize for Commentary in 1976, highlighting his exceptional talent.

A nod of approval from Red Smith showed that he had found something distinctive in Mike Lupica's voice.

There are few topics in this world that can cause more arguments and generate more passion and energy than sports. If you offer an opinion about an athlete, team, coach, or league, you will quickly find yourself under attack from all sides. It's not for the faint of heart, and because of this, Lupica's path hasn't always been smooth, even when he was new to New York.

When he was first covering the New York Knicks, Mike began to write that Walt Frazier, one of the greatest Knicks of all time and one of the greatest players of all time, was slowing down — mostly because he was. "Walt even told some people he thought I might have helped run him out of New York," Mike recalls with a hint of incredulity nearly a half century later. "I always felt that the idea that a twenty-three-year-old could run anybody out of town was pretty funny. But I was just happy they were reading me."

Mike Lupica covered the Knicks for a year at the old *New York Post* and then was offered a column at the *Daily News,* whose editor, Michael O'Neill, was looking for a younger voice in his sports section at the time.

Michael O'Neill took his dear friend Michael Burke — then running the Knicks after a storied career running Ringling Bros. and Barnum & Bailey Circus and the New York Yankees — out to lunch, and asked for some guidance.

"Mike Burke wrote me a long letter about this much later," Mike Lupica says. "He told me Mr. O'Neill had described what he was looking for and Mike Burke said he could give him ten names that fit the bill perfectly. But then Burke said, 'But there's this kid at the *New York Post* who's going to be better than all of them.'"

Mike Lupica's heroes, among them the great Pete Hamill, whose work spanned topics from war to music and everything in between, shaped his approach to his craft, teaching him the power of having a voice. "Pete once said, 'A columnist's voice is like a boxer's left hand. You either have one or don't,'" Mike says. "That

174

always stuck with me, and I always tried to be true to mine."

It's this authenticity that has resonated with readers for years: Whether he's covering the Olympics or Wimbledon, Mike Lupica has a knack for telling it like it is and allowing the words to flow quickly from his mind to his fingertips.

"Pete Hamill also described journalism as history in a hurry," Mike says. "When something big happens, that's it, you sometimes have forty-five minutes and sometimes less to write your own first draft of history." He notes, "I've always thought that the bigger the story, the easier the column was to write. I was in Lake Placid in 1980, the night our Miracle on Ice hockey team shocked the world and beat the Soviets. And I heard a friend of mine in the press room saying, 'How do I write this?' And I told him that the nights when you're trying to make something interesting out of a nothing game are the hard ones, that a game like this was why we all wanted to do this for a living in the first place."

Through his columns, TV appearances, and novels, Mike Lupica has made an indelible mark on sports journalism. His work is a testament to his ability to say something smart and to stay on message in ways that engage readers and viewers alike. He has shown the world how to be nimble and agile and never shy away from sharing an opinion, no matter how contentious it might be.

Embracing Mike Lupica's approach can transform the way you engage in conversations and handle disruptions, and he serves as a great example of positive disrupter behaviors 7 and 8.

Behavior 7: Say Something Smart

Mike Lupica always speaks with intention, offering insights that provoke thought and action. Whether he's critiquing a player's performance or sharing his perspective on a game, his words are always carefully chosen and meaningful. His comments spark conversations as he tackles topics head-on and unapologetically says smart things in his distinctive voice.

Behavior 8: Stay on Message

Whether writing a column, appearing on a television show, or laboring over a book manuscript, Mike Lupica has the ability to stay on message. This consistency has built a trusting and loyal readership that actively seeks out what he has to say about the latest game or the biggest shift in sports. He has proved Red Smith right over the decades — there is something special about what Mike says and how he says it.

Reflect on Your Behaviors

Think of a time when you had something important to say but held back. What was holding you back? And how could you behave differently next time to ensure that your voice is heard?

Recall a discussion or meeting in which the conversation veered off topic. How might you have helped steer it back on course while contributing something of value?

Quick Challenge

In the next discussion or meeting you attend, consciously work to say something smart—something that not only contributes to the conversation but also encourages others to think more deeply or view the issue from a different angle. At the same time, practice staying on message by linking back to the main topic or goal of the conversation, ensuring that it remains productive and focused. This dual approach will not only enhance the quality of your contributions but also model effective communication for others, potentially inspiring them to do the same.

Positive Disrupter Move

Have the Hard Talk

Instead of avoiding it, start it. A small moment of honesty can reshape a whole relationship.

Chapter 20

Heart

Leadership begins with empathy.

Visiting Africa has always been a bucket-list desire for Alicia Wallace, so when the opportunity to travel as part of a medical volunteer trip arises, the recent college graduate jumps at the chance. It's a life-changing experience. Witnessing firsthand the plight of children dying in Sierra Leone—and the mothers desperately caring for them—reshapes Alicia's outlook on life and her sense of purpose.

After returning home, Alicia finds herself struggling with the stark contrast between two worlds. "I learned and saw things that I could not forget," she says.

Disrupted to her core, Alicia can't go back to her previous life working at a Seattle law firm. Despite a personal health crisis of her own, she feels an urgent need to help. "I thought about buying Lululemon yoga pants or going to Starbucks, and I was like, 'I can't do that. Do you know what that money could do for somebody?'" Alicia says. The profound disparity between the daily comforts she once took for granted and the urgent needs of the people she encountered in Sierra Leone isn't about criticizing or judging her fellow Americans; it's simply the nudge she needs to move her passions in a new direction.

The corporate career path she once envisioned for her life is no longer the right one. "I knew I had to do something different," she explains. Embracing the uncertainties of a new journey, Alicia is committed to creating what she calls "real change in the world."

She interviews with a nonprofit organization and has an unexpectedly blunt discussion with the executive director, Gregory Stone, about the best way to provide assistance to impoverished people in Africa. "I don't buy it. I don't believe it," he tells her about what she thinks is a carefully crafted plan. His candid response challenges her, and the two begin a partnership dedicated to creating sustainable job opportunities. "We started creating jobs for men and women locally: farming projects, chicken and egg farms, and pineapple plantations," she says.

Together, they focus on tackling poverty issues at the root, providing underserved communities with the opportunities they need to build their own businesses and shape their own futures. When they discover an export market for artisanal products such as woven baskets, however, Alicia and Greg quickly realize that pivoting to "an exporting model where we could return a high wage [lifts] people out of poverty much faster than a local market model could."

Alicia and Greg cofound All Across Africa, an organization dedicated to supporting skilled African artisans by providing fair hourly wages for their handcrafted products. These artisans create stunning decor items from the safety of their homes, and All Across Africa helps them sell their creations to retail businesses that are committed to making a positive impact.

Their first big sale, in 2013, is to Costco, and thousands of artisans—mostly women—join in creating work for All Across Africa. In exchange for buying the wares in quantities and at prices many times higher than local markets could afford, All Across Africa sets three conditions: The work must be of high quality; the products must be made from local materials; and the artisans' children must all go to school. "The effect is virtuous," Alicia says. "During the first year, the families start eating better, and the second year, their homes are improved. Eventually, they emerge from poverty."

Today, All Across Africa's influence spans the globe. Its artisanal products are available in around 3,500 locations worldwide, including at major retailers such as Target, Ethan Allen, and Anthropologie as well as hundreds of boutiques. More than 6,300 artisans organized into an independent cooperative across Ghana, Rwanda, Uganda, and Tanzania participate in the program and report significant improvements in their lives: 94 percent have investments, 96 percent have children in school, and 88 percent have savings accounts. The life cycle of their products begins with locally grown materials, which are then handcrafted into beautiful decor pieces. These products are sold globally, providing a steady income that supports education, health care, housing, and more in the artisans' communities.

From her initial volunteer experience to becoming a key force for sustainable change in Africa, Alicia's efforts are a testament to the power of behaviors 9 and 10. She has changed many lives—including her own.

Behavior 9: Care About Others

Alicia, moved by the plight of the people she met in Sierra Leone, exemplifies what it means to understand the worries and needs of others and respond with kindness, compassion, and a genuine desire to improve lives. This behavior is vividly illustrated by her dedication to making a substantial impact through her work with African artisans.

Behavior 10: Act on Your Conscience

Acting on your conscience requires courage and sacrifice—a willingness to choose the right path over the easy one. Alicia's decision to shift from a corporate career to one focused on creating sustainable change in Africa is the epitome of this behavior. Despite the complexities and potential risks involved, Alicia chooses to step forward, guided by a moral compass that prioritizes the well-being of others over personal comfort and safety.

Reflect on Your Behaviors

When was the last time you went out of your way to fully understand someone else's challenges or needs?

In choosing between what is easy and what is right, what guides your decisions? How do you align your actions with your values, even if it means making personal sacrifices?

Quick Challenge

Think of a person or a community in need that has touched your heart—perhaps someone close to you, a cause you've read about, or a local community. Take one step within the next week to make a positive impact. Try organizing a small fundraiser, volunteering a few hours of your time, offering your skills, or even starting a conversation and raising awareness about a difficult topic.

Positive Disrupter Move

Name What Matters Today

One sentence a day. What do you care about today? Name it.

Chapter 21

Gut

Make tough calls by trusting your instincts.

Stepping into the role of athletic director at any university is no small feat, but when Chris "Mac" McIntosh takes over at the University of Wisconsin–Madison, in 2021, he isn't just taking on a new job—he's also stepping into the shoes of a legend. Barry Alvarez, the man whose tenure defined Wisconsin Badgers athletics over the previous three decades, has left an indelible mark on the university. Alvarez wasn't just a coach: He was also the architect of a football renaissance, turning a struggling program into a national powerhouse. Under his guidance, the Badgers won three Big Ten titles and claimed three Rose Bowl victories—achievements that transformed not only the football team but also the entire campus culture. For Mac, following in the footsteps of such an iconic figure means carrying forward a tradition of excellence while trying to carve his own path in the shadow of a giant.

Mac has a deep respect for the university, the athletic program, and the towering legacy of Barry Alvarez. He knows the immense pressure that comes with the role, but he also recognizes the importance of trusting his instincts, even when faced with tough decisions. One of the most challenging moments in his early tenure occurs when he decides to part ways with the head football coach, Paul Chryst—a move that sparks widespread controversy and tests his resolve. During his tenure, from 2015 to 2022, Chryst led the Badgers to three Big Ten division titles and several bowl game victories, including in the Cotton Bowl and Orange Bowl. But while Chryst provided stability and success, Mac feels that the program has begun to stagnate.

The decision to replace him with Luke Fickell is a bold move that signals a shift in the football program's direction. Fickell, with his aggressive and adaptable style, brings a fresh perspective, aiming to modernize the team and make it more competitive on the national stage. While there's a risk of disrupting the strong foundation Chryst built, Mac sees the potential reward as significant—a chance to elevate Wisconsin football to new heights under Fickell's forward-thinking leadership.

The decision to release Chryst and bring in Fickell marks a defining moment in Mac's leadership journey and a test of his ability to shepherd an institution through change. "I make decisions...and then you live with the results," Mac asserts, demonstrating his commitment to accountability and integrity.

Mac's guiding principle remains clear: "My goal is to move forward in life or in business or with my family without any regrets," he says. He knows that true leadership often involves making unpopular choices, but his readiness to embrace disruption, combined with his deep understanding of the gravity of his position as athletic director at the University of Wisconsin, defines him as a leader who, despite initial doubts, evolves into a transformative figure.

Mac's journey illustrates the profound impact of gut behaviors — trusting instincts and pushing past butterflies — on positive disruption and leadership. Through his narrative, the power of behaviors 11 and 12 can be seen, essential for modeling resilience and courage and achieving transformation.

Behavior 11: Trust Your Instincts

Mac's tenure proves the importance of listening to your inner voice and trusting your gut, especially when making tough, potentially controversial decisions. This inner guidance is crucial when navigating the complex landscape of college sports. Mac relies on intuition as he leads his organization through turbulent waters.

Behavior 12: Push Past the Butterflies

Facing public scrutiny and doubt, particularly when he makes the difficult decision to release the football coach, Mac embraces the discomfort of moving forward amid uncertainty. This behavior highlights the necessity of confronting nervousness head-on, interpreting it not as a stop sign but as a precursor of significant progress and future success.

Reflect on Your Behaviors

Where in your life or career might you be ignoring your instincts for the sake of playing it safe?

Recall a time when you felt butterflies before making a major decision. How did you push through? And what were the outcomes?

Quick Challenge

Identify a scenario in your life or work that requires you to trust your instincts or push past nervousness. Commit to tackling this challenge within the next week — whether it's making a pivotal decision without clear direction, stepping into a leadership role amid uncertainty, or embarking on a project that sparks internal resistance. Note the shift in your perspective and the growth that ensue after you step out of your comfort zone.

Positive Disrupter Move

Say the Brave "No"

Say "no" with your voice, not just your thoughts. Out loud. Clear. Calm. Done.

Chapter 22

Hands

Feed the body and the spirit.

Chris Whitney is living the dream, running a thriving construction business in St. Louis, Missouri, and cherishing time with family and friends... until life throws him a curveball. His business hits a rough patch, and a frightening prenatal misdiagnosis for his child puts his once stable life into turmoil.

Unexpectedly, Chris and his wife, Elaine, begin to struggle to make ends meet, relying on food pantries to help them feed their family. While the free food during their time of need is sincerely appreciated, the humbling process of standing in line to receive it leaves Chris feeling vulnerable, just another face in a sea of many.

There has to be a better way — one that offers support without stripping away dignity.

Chris finds stability in a new insurance career but is stirred by a deeper calling—one that leads toward a more meaningful path for him, where he can help others in need. The hands that once built buildings are now dedicated to building a brighter future, not only for his family but also for entire communities.

After much research and reflection, Chris and his family pack up and move from Missouri to Tennessee with a single goal: fighting food insecurity. Once they are settled, Chris jumps right into the heart of community service, starting the nonprofit organization One Generation Away with a deep commitment to being hands-on every step of the way. Chris explains that he and Elaine "started out of the back of a Hyundai Santa Fe," rescuing food from the alley behind a grocery store. It is a simple beginning but proves to be fuel for the fire of his mission to ensure that perfectly good food ends up not in landfills but on the tables of people in need.

Chris's efforts take a monumental leap forward, thanks to a seemingly simple yet transformative suggestion. A stranger suggests to Elaine that she and Chris "bring a 53-foot trailer full of food to a parking lot," where the couple could feed people out of it. The idea sparks a significant expansion of One Generation Away's operations, but just as Chris makes real progress on his vision, signing his first lease on a warehouse where he can store the food, another disruption is thrown on the path.

In December 2013, he notices a little bump on his neck. The diagnosis: stage 3 throat cancer.

Chris views the health issue not as a setback but as a season of life.

"Disruption doesn't define me," he declares. "It's not the end, it's not the beginning, and it could be a catalyst for something greater than you can ever dream."

Through Chris Whitney's leadership and the unwavering commitment of the One Generation Away team, what began with a single car packed with unused food in an alleyway has blossomed into a substantial movement. Despite his ups and downs, continuing to stay in the fight makes all the difference. "We dropped 50 percent in production over the next year. But now, from there to where we are today, ten years later, is just one of the most unbelievable stories." One Generation Away has soared to remarkable heights: Its operations extend across three states, and it distributes more than ten million pounds of food to people in need.

Chris emphasizes the vital role that relationships and family play in living a good life. "Family is everything," he says. "Without the support of my wife and children, it's nearly impossible to create and fulfill my vision of meaningful change and impact."

Having people who are passionate about the cause

and can carry the mission forward is essential. "Family and relationships are the foundation," he says. "They're what not only launch your disruptive idea but also help you stay the course." And they're crucial when navigating disruption. "You need people who have the permission to tell you the truth," he explains. "These are the relationships that lift you up on the days when discouragement creeps in, and you feel like giving up. They're also the voices that keep your ego in check during moments of success, ensuring that it's never just about you, but about the collective 'we' and the mission at hand."

This story not only underscores the significant impact on societal well-being of perseverance, community support, and innovative ideas but also highlights the transformative power of viewing life's disruptions as opportunities for growth and greater achievements, of letting go of something good in order to grab something better, and getting your hands dirty in the process. Another way to look at it is to consider behaviors 13 and 14 of a positive disrupter as opportunities for growth and greater achievements.

Behavior 13: Let Go of Good to Get Better

Picture your hands as the tools you use to shape the future. Sometimes you've got to let go of what you're holding to snatch up something even bigger. It's about recognizing the right moment to step away from the comfort of the known and leap toward opportunities that push you further. Chris did this when he and his family decided to leave the life they knew in St. Louis and pursue a higher calling in Tennessee.

Behavior 14: Get Your Hands Dirty

Here's the deal: Your hands are meant for the tough stuff. Embrace the hard work, the sweat, and the determination needed to turn your aspirations into achievements. Backing down from a challenge? That's not in the playbook. It's the hard, hands-on work that turns your dreams into reality. Chris embodied this from the first food item he picked up in the alleyway to his willingness to battle cancer. His story is one of hand-to-hand combat.

If you're struggling to make a change, start by taking on smaller challenges that aren't too intimidating. Then you can gradually build up your grit and determination, just like you might build up a particular set of muscles at the gym.

Reflect on Your Behaviors

Do you generally find it hard to let go of something good for a chance at reaching for something better? If so, you may be holding yourself back from opportunities in both your personal and professional life. Think hard about whether you've truly chosen your current situation—or whether you've merely gotten stuck.

Quick Challenge

Identify a task or project you've been avoiding, especially one that seems daunting because of potential disruptions or its demand for hard work. This could be a project that could transform your work environment, a personal goal you've put off, or an adaptation to a recent disruption. Roll up your sleeves, grab hold of one task, and do it this week.

~~~~~~

Positive Disrupter Move

Question It

Before reacting, pause and ask: "What if I'm wrong?" One breath, one question, total game-changer.

~~~~~~

Chapter 23

Feet

Wisdom is more important than intelligence.

In the early light of a Miami morning, Jeff Campbell sits in his car, heart pounding, as the radio crackles with breaking news: His company, Burger King, is about to be hit with a major lawsuit from its biggest competitors.

The reason? Jeff himself.

How did Jeff find himself at the center of this storm?

It all began in a pivotal meeting at Burger King's ad agency, J. Walter Thompson. Jeff isn't looking for just another safe, run-of-the-mill marketing campaign. He's after something daring—something that will not only promote the brand but also shake up the entire industry. "I was pretty brash," he confesses. He throws out

the existing campaign, looks the agency's creative director in the eye — yes, that creative director, James Patterson — and boldly declares, "I don't want just any
generic campaign. If that's the idea, toss it in the trash.
I want something bold, something that puts the product front and center."

Jeff is convinced that Burger King's future depends
on a marketing strategy that breaks all the rules. "The
first thing I did was tell Patterson and the others at J.
Walter Thompson, 'We need a campaign built entirely
around the product. That's the direction we're going.'"
This demand for a product-centric approach sets the
stage for what will become one of the most audacious
moves in advertising history.

The result?

The infamous "Battle of the Burgers" campaign —
a no-holds-barred challenge to the competition that
sends shock waves through both the fast-food and advertising industries. Attack ads had previously been used
in political campaigns, but not for mass-market products like hamburgers. Yet here was Burger King claim-
ing flat out that their burgers were more delicious.

"We saw McDonald's as the equivalent of the
Antichrist back then, and they felt the same about us,"
Jeff says knowingly, underscoring the fierce rivalry
that fuels the campaign. As a direct result of the ads,

McDonald's files a lawsuit (later settled) alleging false advertising...but the publicity only heightens the "Battle of the Burgers" and boosts Burger King's sales.

Jeff goes all in. His actions aren't just bold—they're also the epitome of positive disruption, perfectly illustrating behaviors 15 and 16. The risk is enormous, but so is the potential reward.

Behavior 15: Run Toward Disruption

The Burger King ad campaign is not just a shift in advertising tactics; it's also a full-on sprint toward change, embracing innovation and setting a new standard for the ways in which companies can engage with their competition. It pits Burger King against its biggest rival—throwing down the gauntlet!

Behavior 16: Stand Firm Despite Doubters

Anticipating the backlash from McDonald's was a calculated risk. "We knew, or we thought we knew, that if we did that, McDonald's would sue us," Jeff remarks. This readiness to face legal challenges head-on exemplifies behavior 16: standing firm in the face of doubters. The lawsuit that ensues tests Jeff's resolve but ultimately vindicates his disruptive approach. The resulting publicity underscores the effectiveness of pushing back against opposition, proving that daring to be different can lead to unprecedented success.

The campaign not only survives the legal challenge but also thrives, generating an estimated $100 million worth of free publicity and igniting a series of independent taste tests that reinforce the brand's claims of superior quality. This series of events marks a significant departure from traditional marketing strategies, showcasing the power of sticking to one's convictions, even in the face of significant doubt and opposition.

Reflect on Your Behaviors

Can you identify a time when embracing change led to unexpected or transformative outcomes in your life or career?

How do you deal with doubt from within or from other people when pursuing a new idea or direction?

Quick Challenge

Identify an aspect of your professional or personal life that would benefit from change or innovation, such as a project at work, a personal goal, or a routine that needs revitalizing. Anticipate resistance or skepticism from others and even from within yourself. Consider strategies to maintain your resolve and stay committed

to your bold, disruptive move. Keep the potential transformative outcomes in mind and stay motivated and
focused.

Positive Disrupter Move

Pause Before You Pounce

Ask, "Is this mine to carry, fix, or say right now?"

Quick Recap: Behave

The lessons of moving from discernment to action:

- Success is achieved through actions, routines, and behaviors.
- Each disruptive role requires effort and resilience.
- Surround yourself with complementary powers: leverage others' strengths to compensate for your weaknesses.

For ease of recall, the chart on the next page organizes the Anatomy of a Positive Disrupter as a series of behaviors associated with parts of the body.

The Anatomy of a Positive Disrupter

Brain		Heart	
1	Think deeply to uncover insights	9	Care about others
2	Believe better is possible	10	Act on your conscience
Eyes		**Gut**	
3	Have a vision	11	Trust your instincts
4	See brutal reality	12	Push past the butterflies
Ears		**Hands**	
5	Listen to understand	13	Let go of good to get better
6	Hear what's not said	14	Get your hands dirty
Mouth		**Feet**	
7	Say something smart	15	Run toward disruption
8	Stay on message	16	Stand firm despite doubters

Disrupting Beyond Yourself

The best positive disrupters know how to harness the collective abilities of their families, teams, and organizations to explore options and deliver results.

Tapping into the strengths of positive disrupter behaviors is where the magic of collective brilliance happens.

Part V
Achieve

Chapter 24

Disruptive Impact

Examine the polar opposite of conventional thinking.

Jazz is the sound of surprise within a surrounding structure, and for Josh Linkner, it's also the sound of renewal within a disruptive structure in Detroit.

"I'm from here, and I'm very passionate about the city. I've had the chance to leave many times, but I've always wanted to stay," Josh says. He's gone from sneaking into Motor City jazz clubs in his younger years in the hope of performing onstage to becoming an active participant in Detroit's remarkable resurgence through his support of entrepreneurs in the city.

After years of success as the hub of the automotive industry, Detroit became a punch line, a symbol of urban decay. The lack of overall economic diversity led to a bloated governmental bureaucracy and financial malaise. "We got caught up in our ways and became very bureaucratic, and our city suffered. Our disruptive mojo went away," Josh laments. But he sees potential where others see defeat.

Josh's role in Detroit's rebirth stems from his entrepreneurial spirit. In 2010, he founds Detroit Venture Partners with the goal of not only making money but also making a difference in the lives of entrepreneurs trying to launch their businesses. "Everyone thought we were crazy. They said, 'Go to Silicon Valley,' but we wanted to do it in Detroit," he says. Since 2010, Detroit Venture Partners has helped grow Detroit's entrepreneurial community by backing and funding more than ninety early-stage technology companies.

His efforts pay off. Detroit Venture Partners is a catalyst in the city's entrepreneurial ecosystem, supporting businesses that are now integral to Detroit's economy. "We started to see a pivot to something much more," Josh says. His experience as a jazz musician influences his approach. "Jazz is a balance between structure and freedom. There's a framework—a key, a time signature—but within that, there's immense room for creativity...Leadership today needs a similar balance. Too strict, and you stifle creativity; too loose, and there's chaos. You need enough structure to keep things organized but enough freedom to innovate."

In 2021, he continues his disruptive efforts by starting

Mudita Venture Partners with his brother, Ethan. "Mudita means taking joy in other people's success," he explains. This firm invests in early-stage tech companies in Detroit, fostering an environment where innovation thrives.

Detroit is no longer just about building bigger and better cars; it's now about mobility, corporate finance, and more. "The two largest mortgage companies are in Detroit," Josh points out, highlighting the city's expanding economic base. "What's happening now is a beautiful rebirth. This once broken city is rising from the ashes," he says. He strongly believes Detroit's turnaround will be studied for decades as one of the great American comeback stories. "We're finally getting back to being disruptive. Now there's economic diversity. People are trying new stuff and injecting creativity in unexpected places," he adds. The city is witnessing a renaissance with thriving music, food, and art scenes.

Josh's story illustrates the impact of positive disrupters and his beliefs about disruption align with the message: "All human beings are creative. All humans have the capacity to be disruptive for good. Absolutely, yes! Full stop!"

Josh disrupted himself by transitioning from a career as a jazz musician to a life as a venture capitalist. He disrupted his business by fostering a collaborative and innovative culture. He disrupted his work by challenging the status quo in the technology and investment sectors and helping people see that tech has a home in Detroit. He disrupted his family—notably, his brother, Ethan—by involving them in his mission. And finally, he disrupted his community by playing a role in Detroit's revival from manufacturing to creativity and commerce.

Just as jazz has a structure—keys, time signatures, and themes—so does the process of positive disruption. In this book, that structure, including roles to play (Trailblazer, Torchbearer, and others) and behaviors to adopt (think deeply to uncover insights, believe better is possible, and so on) have been laid out. Now you can explore the ways in which your efforts will achieve results for your families, teams, organizations, industries, business relationships, and beyond.

Areas of Disruptive Impact

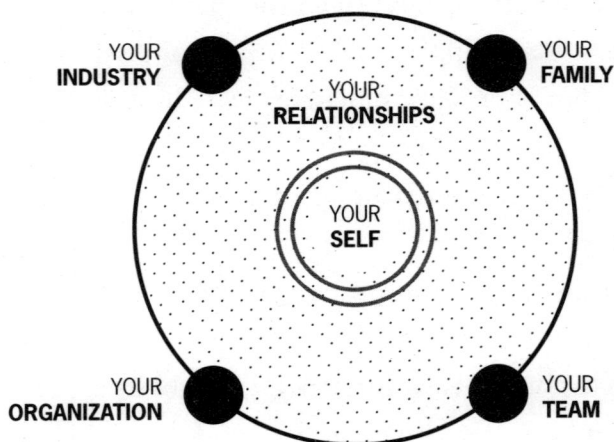

This Areas of Disruptive Impact model places you at the center because every meaningful change begins with disrupting yourself. Consider where your own disruptive efforts might take you, and the people around you.

The shifts that truly matter—in your family, your work, and beyond—start within. You're surrounded by a web of relationships, both personal and professional, and you have the power to transform those connections for the better. From there, your impact can grow from one-on-one interactions to influencing your family, your team, your organization, your industry, and even beyond.

Positive Disrupter Move

Reset the Room

Bad energy? Heavy vibe? Pause and say, "Let's reset." Simple words. Big shift.

Chapter 25
Disrupt Your Relationships

Reinvent relationships to reach new heights.

At Mount Everest's South Base Camp, eighteen-year-old Lucy Westlake and her father, Rodney, share an emotional farewell. The icy winds carry their words away, but the bond forged during a decade of shared adventures holds strong.

Reaching the base camp, located at an elevation of 17,598 feet, is a significant goal itself and appears on many people's bucket lists, but it also marks a turning point. As they trek through the rugged Himalayan terrain, Rodney reflects that his daughter, his trusted climbing partner for so long, is now moving on without him.

"I started mountain climbing when I was seven," Lucy recalls. "We would travel on family road trips and stop along the way, get out of the car, and hike a high point—that's when you climb the highest natural elevation in a state. As the mountains became bigger, my mom and younger brother would stay in the car or in a hotel, and it became my dad's and my adventure to climb these mountains." After several trips, the duo has racked up a lot of mountains.

"I was the dreamer; my parents were the planners," Lucy says. Rodney agrees. "Lucy's job was to be physically fit enough to do the hard work and mentally tough enough to actually climb the mountains. My job was essentially to figure out the routes. To figure out how we were going to not only travel to the mountains but up the mountains," he says. Lucy's mom—his wife, Amy—is responsible for organizing the gear.

"The level of trust was very intense early on," Rodney says. "Especially when Lucy was not quite strong enough to wield an ice ax or set her crampons. As a result, we had to adapt our approach as we traversed ice. We had many discussions about how to work together and trust one another. At first, it was tough to trust her to the point where my life was in her hands, but over time, her skills grew, and our relationship strengthened."

After several years of hiking adventures, Lucy sets a world record as the youngest female to climb all forty-eight high points in the continental United States and sets the record for youngest father-daughter duo. Next on the list is a trip to Hawaii, where they knock its high point off their list.

Then it's down to one more mountain: Denali (also known as Mount McKinley).

Referred to as "the Great One," Denali, in Alaska, is North America's highest peak, at 20,310 feet.

Denali poses a significant challenge for the thirteen-year-old climber and her father. Over the course of three weeks on the mountain, they hike, sleep in tents, wait out bad weather, and support each other through physical and mental highs and lows. "We'd climbed some big mountains including Mount Kilimanjaro, the highest in Africa. Other ones were also very challenging, like Mount Rainier in Washington, Gannett in Wyoming, and Granite in Montana. But Denali was a whole different beast," Lucy recalls. "We were expected to each carry about 100 pounds. And I weighed about 100 pounds. I still weigh about 100 pounds. So that was very challenging."

The mountain's unpredictable nature thwarts their plans. After spending weeks on the mountain, they have only a three-day window in which to summit, but the weather—and a fatality among other climbers—makes it impossible.

"We had never failed to summit before that mountain. It was a shock," says Lucy. "It took a while for me to even want to go back to Denali. But finally, I kind of got the itch again, and I started bugging my parents to go back."

The itch isn't just about summiting more mountains; it's much more than that. Lucy yearns for the time with her dad, the bonds they form, and the way they team up to accomplish something together. It's about their relationship.

Four years later, they tackle Denali again. Once again, weather is a factor. Most of the team is ready to call it quits. As Lucy says, "Success in mountain climbing isn't determined by getting to the top of the mountain, but by safely getting off the mountain." Looking at the weather window, Rodney and Lucy have a tough choice to make — keep going or join the rest of the team and pack it out.

Father and daughter discuss their options. Years of mountaineering together have given the pair the skills and experience to tackle the mountain and the trust and resolve to do it together. The two of them set out by themselves in the early hours and soon reach their goal of standing on top of North America. It's a testament to their hard work and determination — and it sets a new record: Rodney and Lucy are the youngest father-daughter team to reach all fifty states' high points.

Soon it's time for their relationship to evolve.

At the Mount Everest base camp, Rodney chooses

not to ascend while Lucy sets out with her new climbing partner, Mingma Chhiring Sherpa.

It's a pivotal moment. Rodney steps back while Lucy and her new partner move forward together. Reflecting on this turning point, Rodney acknowledges, "I knew it was time for our relationship to evolve."

Lucy's successful navigation through the perilous Khumbu Icefall and her ultimate summit to 29,032 feet on May 12, 2023, at the age of eighteen, made her the youngest US female to ever reach the top of Everest.

The story of Lucy and Rodney Westlake is a profound example of the way personal and professional relationships can evolve and thrive through disruption. Their journey underscores the importance of setting goals together, taking small steps toward big accomplishments, maintaining transparency, being candid with one another, and cultivating mutual trust. It also highlights the significance of knowing when to step back and allow others to reach new heights—a delicate balance that strengthens bonds and opens new paths for growth.

But of course you don't have to climb Mount Everest to create meaningful disruption.

While Lucy and Rodney's story unfolds on some of the world's tallest mountains, for those staying closer to sea level, Joel Peterson offers another example of the importance of navigating peaks — this time in the business world. He has served as the chairman of the board of JetBlue Airways Corporation, taught students at the Stanford Graduate School of Business, and built his own multibillion-dollar private equity firm. He's purchased more than three hundred companies during his five-decade career and along the way has faced many disruptions — broken business relationships, unforeseen lawsuits, disgruntled team members. Joel has learned that navigating these situations requires clarity of roles, a desire to build trust, and a willingness to disrupt relationships for the better.

His focus is on what he calls "solving for fair." This philosophy requires him to put aside assumptions, ask questions, listen to understand, and say no to deals and relationships that aren't mutually beneficial. Joel knows that getting into business with someone who isn't looking for a mutually beneficial relationship or ignoring character issues to close a deal are recipes for disaster. Things like these don't get better over time — they get worse.

Both Lucy and Rodney's mountaineering and Joel's business climbs highlight the fact emphasized in Chapter 5: Relationships provide both headwinds and tailwinds.

In pursuit of your good life, you must work to build trust, seek mutual respect, and disrupt relationships for the better.

Looking to Disrupt Your Relationships? Here Are a Few Places to Start

Disrupting a relationship, whether personal or professional, can be one of the most challenging yet rewarding things you can do. Evaluating and disrupting relationships can lead to growth and stronger connections. Following are some key points to consider, inspired by the story of Lucy and Rodney Westlake.

Clearly Define Roles and Mutual Benefit: In the beginning, Rodney led his climbs with Lucy, handling logistics and carrying the bulk of the load while Lucy focused on physical preparation. As time passed, their roles evolved, and they became equal partners in both physical and mental preparation. Eventually, Lucy forged a new path and continued on her journey without Rodney. Their story highlights the importance of clearly defining roles in relationships and ensuring that each person contributes and benefits in ways that align with their strengths and needs.

Set and Work Toward Shared Goals: Lucy and Rodney's goal to climb the highest points in all fifty states started as a casual family activity and grew into a significant achievement. Setting and working toward shared goals strengthened their bond. Establish common goals and work toward them together. Regularly review and adjust these goals to keep the relationship dynamic and forward-moving.

Build Trust: Trust was paramount for Lucy and Rodney, especially in dangerous situations such as navigating crevasses on Denali. They relied on each other for safety and support. Build and maintain trust by being reliable, transparent, and supportive. Trust is the foundation of any strong relationship and needs continual nurturing.

Show Commitment and Loyalty: Despite the challenges, Lucy and Rodney remained committed to their goals and to each other, even when facing setbacks such as their initial failure on Denali. Show commitment through actions and words. Loyalty and dedication strengthen relationships, especially during tough times.

Foster Transparency and Communication: Lucy and Rodney had to communicate openly about their physical and mental states, particularly in life-threatening situations. Foster open communication. Be honest about your feelings and encourage others to do the same. Clear and candid communication can prevent misunderstandings and build deeper connections.

Evaluate Relationship Dynamics: Lucy and Rodney's relationship evolved from that of parent and child to a partnership of equals. They had to adapt and grow together. Regularly assess your relationships. Identify those that are strong and worth maintaining. Determine which ones might benefit from disruption to stay healthy, those that need intervention to get back on track, and those that might need to end.

Handle Tough Conversations: Facing the decision to continue their climb without their team required difficult conversations and tough decisions on Lucy and Rodney's part. Approach tough conversations with kindness and openness. Be prepared to listen as much as you speak. These candid, one-on-one exchanges are crucial for growth and clarity in any relationship.

Positive Disrupter Move

Grab the Takeaway

Before the day ends, name one insight, lesson, or reminder you gained. Just one. Write it down, say it out loud, or carry it forward. Don't leave today empty-handed.

Remember Trina Frierson's story in Chapter 5 and the fact that relationships can act as either headwinds or tailwinds? Revisit that insight and refer to "Tool 5: Analyze Your Relationships" in "Part VII: Your Positive Disrupter Toolkit."

Chapter 26

Disrupt Your Family: A Personal Story from Patrick Leddin

The four walls of our homes contain life's most important relationships.

They say that sometimes, a dying person waits to pass away until the last loved one arrives. In my mom's case, it seems I'm the one she's waiting for. Late one night, after a long journey, my wife, Jamie, and I finally arrive at my parents' house, in Chicago. When we walk in, my mom rallies. She's alert and engaged. We spend precious time together.

A few hours later, she passes.

In the days that follow, our family is caught in a whirlwind of funeral arrangements and family gatherings. Eventually things quiet down, and I am able to consider how different this moment would have felt had I not made a decision eighteen months previously that changed everything.

It all starts with a meeting I attend at which the speaker asks us to think about the roles we play in life—parent, partner, friend, leader, and more. She asks us to ponder which roles matter most. I list twenty roles I'm juggling and narrow it down to the six that feel most important. One role I pick is that of son. Then we're asked to assess how well we're doing in each role.

When I look at my results, I realize I'm doing okay in most areas, but my assessment of the son role stops me in my tracks. In all honesty, my interactions with my parents have become stale, driven more by obligation than connection. I'll call them once a week, but our conversations are mostly surface-level: updates on the weather, traffic reports, and a rundown of my schedule. Then I'll hang up the phone and move on with my day. A not-uncommon situation, one in which family relationships feel more like a task to check off than a meaningful interaction.

That realization hits hard, and I vow to do something different. I think about how busy my wife and I are raising our kids. My parents raised five kids: I figure they have some wisdom to offer, so I start asking them for advice in our weekly calls. They know a lot. I also begin sending them postcards from my travels, small gestures that help reignite our connection.

Over time, I feel myself doing better as a son, and our relationship strengthens.

Then comes the call from my brother. I'm on a business trip when he tells me, "Mom is sick. You need to come home." I say I'll be there in a few days, but he insists, "No—you need to come now." I turn around, fly home, pick up Jamie, and drive straight to Chicago. I make it just in time.

After the funeral, we gather at what is now just my dad's house. The room feels heavy with my mom's absence. I turn to Jamie and say, "I'm so glad I did that assessment and decided to be a better son." She nods toward my dad and reminds me, "You're still a son."

I love my dad very much, but he has always been a tough guy. While my mom was the "yes" parent, he was the "no" parent. I'm not thrilled with Jamie's nudge, but I walk across the room and say, "Hey, Dad. I travel a lot for work. Would you ever want to come with me?"

I fully expect him to decline, but instead he asks, "Where are you going?"

Flustered, I check my schedule and say, "Topeka, Kansas, in two weeks."

Two weeks later, my dad comes to Topeka.

That trip changes everything. We share a flight, a hotel room, and several meals. He watches me give a presentation to an audience and for the first time gets a glimpse into my professional life. I see him in a new light, too. Yes, he was the "no" guy and could be tough to connect with, but he worked tirelessly—holding multiple jobs as a telephone installer, bartender, and more—while raising five kids on the south side of Chicago.

Since then, we've taken more trips together, deepening our bond in a way I never considered possible.

As I write this, my mom has been gone fourteen years, and my dad is ninety-four. I'm grateful I took the time to take stock of where I stood and chose to reignite the fire between me and my parents.

It's never too late to disrupt your family.

I don't claim to be a family therapist. Still, I do know that at the end of life—after work is over and the accolades of our professional careers have set with the sun—what will remain is our family relationships. Use this chapter to disrupt your family dynamics for the better. If there are strained relationships, perhaps today is the day to change that. If trust is broken, now might be the time to fix it. If the people around your dinner table—if you even have one of those—have become strangers, now is the time to disrupt your family.

No matter your family situation—whether you have a house full of kids or none at all; whether you live in a bustling city or a quiet country setting; whether you have stay-at-home parents or working ones—the lesson here is universal.

In life, the most important relationships are often those within the four walls of our homes. Unfortunately, these are often the very relationships that are undervalued, underserved, and suffering.

Looking to Disrupt Your Family? Here Are a Few Places to Start

When one member of a family faces change, that person becomes the disrupter. His or her individual decisions affect everyone. Remember the dilemma Megan Piphus described in Chapter 1. The experience of being a young mother looking to change careers posed a major disruption to her family.

"It was a hard balance having a full-time job in real estate and also starting a career at *Sesame Street*. I have a family and two young children," she said, as she weighed her choices. "I just needed to take a leap of faith to move into the television industry and puppetry full-time."

She could have put her dreams on hold to preserve the comfort of stability and routine. Instead, she chose to move forward into the unknown. "Within a couple of weeks of leaving my career in real estate, the news broke about me being the first Black woman puppeteer on *Sesame Street*."

Here are actions to take as you consider change that affects those you care for most.

Clarify Your Family Values: Just as you have a fire inside yourself, consider the fire that burns inside your family. What values do you collectively stand for? What do you hope to achieve together? How will you nurture and treat one another? What message do you want to share with the world about who you are as a family?

Prioritize Family Time: Schedule regular family activities or meals at which everyone can connect without distractions. Spend quality time together.

Open the Lines of Communication: Create an environment where all family members feel safe expressing their thoughts and feelings. This can help address underlying issues and foster stronger relationships. As I found with my dad, it's never too late to make this shift.

Support One Another's Goals: Encourage and assist family members in pursuing their individual goals and dreams, and remember that their dreams aren't always your dreams for them—and that's okay.

Reevaluate Priorities: Assess what truly matters

to you and your family. Be willing to make significant changes if it means aligning more closely with your core values; though, as I discovered when I started to reconnect with my parents, sometimes even relatively small changes can help realign your priorities.

Show Appreciation: Regularly express gratitude and appreciation for each family member. This can strengthen bonds and create a more positive family environment.

Invest in Personal Growth: Encourage continual learning and personal development. This can help everyone grow together and support one another's journeys.

Address and Heal Past Conflicts: Take proactive steps to resolve any lingering conflicts or issues. Forgiveness and understanding can pave the way for healthier relationships.

Create New Traditions: Establish new family traditions that everyone can look forward to and participate in. This can create lasting memories and reinforce family unity.

Be Present: Make a conscious effort to be mentally and emotionally present during family interactions. Genuine presence can significantly enhance the quality of your relationships. What good is a weekly phone call if it's completely superficial and routine? It's so much better to ask questions with heartfelt curiosity, and then *really listen* to the answers.

Lead by Example: Demonstrate the behaviors and values you want to see in other people. Show your commitment to family and set a powerful example for others to follow.

~~~~~~

Positive Disrupter Move

Reach Out First

Don't wait. Be the one who texts, calls, or checks in.

~~~~~~

Chapter 27
Disrupt Your Team

Building successful teams transforms the lives of its members.

Walking into Basketball Hall of Fame Coach John Calipari's office in Memorial Coliseum on the University of Kentucky campus is a tremendous experience. The typical workplace vibe is quickly replaced by a palpable sense of history and achievement. One wall is adorned with basketballs, each representing a significant win or milestone. Another is covered in photos. A third wall showcases National Collegiate Basketball Hall of Fame memorabilia. The fourth is a glass wall, offering a view into the team's practice facility.

Division I of the NCAA is always a pressure cooker, and the world in which John Calipari operates is being disrupted faster than perhaps any other sports environment out there. Coach Cal's approach to leadership and disruption starts by realistically understanding where he stands and the challenges he faces. "At UMass, you're disrupting everything by getting to the semifinals of the national tournament. That is a total disruption," he says, reflecting on his time as head basketball coach at the University of Massachusetts, from 1988 to 1996. During his time there, he led the team to five Atlantic 10 Conference tournament championships and five Atlantic 10 Conference regular-season titles, culminating in a Final Four appearance in 1996.

His success at UMass is a testament to his innovative coaching style and his ability to build a cohesive team from diverse talent. This period marks Coach Cal's transition from his previous assistant roles to that of head coach, in which he demonstrates his ability to elevate a lower-division program to national prominence. It's also a period when his team faces sanctions over questions of NCAA rule violations — and though painful, marks a pivot point in his coaching career that takes him from college basketball to the National Basketball Association, coaching the New Jersey Nets for three years before returning to college athletics at the University of Memphis in 2000.

Coach Cal's next tenure is characterized by remarkable success and further evolution of his disruptive

228

strategies. "We were good, but Derrick Rose took us to another place," he says, highlighting the transformative impact of star players. Memphis becomes a powerhouse under Calipari's leadership, consistently competing at the highest levels. He guides the team to four Conference USA tournament championships and five Conference USA regular-season titles, earning a Final Four appearance in 2008. The highlight of this period is winning the National Invitational Tournament championship in 2002.

In 2009, Coach Cal joins the University of Kentucky. "When I came here, it was a different deal. I could recruit multiple kids that would have an opportunity to be one-and-done," he says, referring to the phenomenon in college basketball in which a student plays a single year at a university before joining the NBA. There are two sides to that coin: On the one hand, a team gets an amazing athlete, but on the other, that star player will be gone before the next season. It creates significant challenges when trying to build a team.

His approach is not to avoid the challenge but to embrace it. At the University of Kentucky, he chooses to focus on player-first strategies and embrace the one-and-done phenomenon. His tactics result in several Final Four appearances and a national title in 2012. "By taking that approach, we went from an Elite Eight one year and losing eight guys from the team to the NBA to the next year taking a new team to the Final Four," he recounts. "The next year, we lost most of that team. Three guys come back; two freshmen come back. We bring in freshmen, and that team wins a national title." Calipari leads the Kentucky Wildcats to six Southeastern Conference tournament championships and six Southeastern Conference regular-season titles.

Coach Cal's ability to consistently rebuild and guide his teams to success earns him numerous accolades, including Naismith College Coach of the Year in 1996, 2008, and 2015 and AP College Coach of the Year in 2015. He doesn't hesitate to invite the best talent to join the team but ensures that they share its values. One of his key strategies is adapting his leadership to fit the players' strengths and weaknesses rather than forcing them into a rigid system.

Leaning forward in his seat with intensity and enthusiasm, he speaks about the success of his players and how his approach ensures that young athletes are prepared for the NBA and life beyond basketball. "About 70 percent of the players that accept scholarships here get drafted," he notes. "Of that number, 73 percent get to third deals. That's generational, life-changing success at that point."

John Calipari now faces a new disruption. After

fifteen years at the University of Kentucky, he is named the head coach of the University of Arkansas men's basketball team. When Coach Cal arrived at Arkansas for the 2024–25 season, he walked into a mess. The team was coming off a losing year, the fans were restless, and the roster had holes all over it. Expectations were sky-high — but the foundation was shaky. So what did he do? He got to work. Brought in fresh talent, built a new culture, and gave the team an identity. Sure, they stumbled early — starting SEC play 0–5 — but then they caught fire. Arkansas finished 22–14 and fought their way to the Sweet Sixteen.

Just like that, Razorback basketball had swagger again. And as college athletics continues to evolve, Coach Cal remains focused on his mission: transforming young lives and building successful teams. Reflecting the ever-changing landscape, he opts to be enthusiastic about where things will go.

Coach Cal realizes that no matter what changes in college basketball, his focus needs to be on his team, his players, and the legacy they are building together. "My dad was a baggage handler. Mom worked at the high school cafeteria." He's mindful of what success can mean for his players, and his role in helping them achieve it. "I can change the lives of families while I'm in this seat," he adds. "It moves me."

Looking to Disrupt Your Team?
Here Are a Few Places to Start

John Calipari's story of disrupting teams and winning championships holds valuable lessons for people looking to make a significant impact in their work or personal lives. Remember: you don't have to be the team leader to help create a disruptive shift.

Clarify the Purpose of Your Team: As we noted about your family, consider that your team also has a collective fire that burns inside them. Of course you want to win — whatever winning looks like in your world — but what values do you collectively stand for? How will you nurture and treat one another? What message do you want to share with the world about *how* you won, not merely the fact that you won?

Stay Flexible and Open to Change: Adjust your strategies as needed to meet new challenges and adapt to the strengths and weaknesses of your team. Coach Cal and his staff have had to adjust many times: to new players, new NCAA rules, and even, when he moved to the University of Arkansas, a new school.

Focus on Team Values: Prioritize the development and well-being of your team members. Ensure that the talent you bring on board shares the values of the team, because their success will ultimately drive your collective achievements. Coach Cal expects everyone's behavior to align with those values, both on and off the court.

Make Bold Decisions: Even when decisions are difficult, focus on long-term benefits rather than short-term gains. Be willing to adjust your leadership style to fit the needs and goals of your team. Like Coach Cal, you may need to try a new approach for the first time in the middle of a high-stakes game.

Set High Goals: Aim for ambitious targets. High goals inspire teams to push beyond their limits and achieve excellence. Coach Cal begins each season envisioning nothing less than an NCAA tournament championship.

Emphasize Hard Work: Success often comes from relentless effort and dedication. Encourage diligence and persistence in your team. Talent alone will get you only so far.

Implement Effective Systems: Put systems and processes in place that support the team's objectives. Effective systems help teams operate smoothly and achieve their goals efficiently.

Build Strong Habits: Focus on day-to-day execution by building strong habits, committing to hard work, and continually striving to improve. A consistent effort that emphasizes routine and repetition leads to long-term success.

Staying flexible and open to change, focusing on team values, making bold decisions, setting high goals, emphasizing hard work, implementing effective systems, and building strong habits can drive significant change and lead your team to unprecedented success. John Calipari's success teaches that great leaders adapt to the needs of their team members, not the other way around, and understand the importance of delivering results in the moment while helping team members become the best versions of themselves.

Positive Disrupter Move

Walk It Off

Put down the phone. Move your body. Let your mind reset.

Chapter 28
Disrupt Your Organization

Make bold pivots in response to opportunities and crises.

Disrupting an organization can be more challenging than disrupting yourself, your family, or a small team. But you will find that it's often essential in order to capitalize on opportunities or survive crises. Even when disruption comes at you hard and fast, if you can connect the dots between your personal and professional lives, you can thrive in both.

You can find something extraordinary by leaning into the unexpected.

When disruption hits like a freight train, it's hard to think about gradual improvement. When you face a shock like the COVID-19 pandemic, artificial intelligence, or new leadership that wants to change all the rules, you can either adapt *right now* or fall behind.

Let's dive into two real-world examples: one in which disruption was forced on a company and another in which a company chose to disrupt itself. In both stories, leaders didn't merely react—they instead took charge, reshaped their visions, rallied their people, and turned disruption into a catalyst for growth. They proved that disruption can spark powerful transformations, for both individuals and entire organizations.

Disruption Thrust upon You: Tractor Supply's Pandemic Pivot

When COVID-19 hits, the global disruption dramatically reshapes the way people live. As many people relocate to rural or exurban areas and embrace country living, they start growing their own food, raising backyard chickens, and taking on DIY projects that turn their homes into personal sanctuaries.

Tractor Supply Company, declared an essential business, is well-positioned to meet these emerging needs. CEO Hal Lawton and his team quickly note a surge in demand, particularly from millennials new to rural living. These customers have questions, and Tractor Supply's team members are ready to provide answers and guidance.

Hal's leadership is marked by three key traits: listening, empowering, and prioritizing. Recognizing the market shift, he empowers his team to deliver solutions. With more than 2,200 stores in forty-nine states and a workforce of more than fifty thousand, Tractor Supply has been serving the rural lifestyle market for more than eighty-five years. Within just two weeks, the company rolls out same-day delivery across all two-thousand-plus stores, soon followed by curbside pickup. These innovations transform the customer experience, making it easier for homeowners to access the products they need.

On the technology front, Tractor Supply introduces AI-powered earpieces for employees. Initially designed to reduce contact during the pandemic, over time they become essential, providing instant information to employees and helping them offer faster and more informed customer service.

But Hal's focus isn't just on operations; he's also investing in his people. In June of 2020, every hourly team member receives a one-dollar-an-hour raise, and the company updates its benefits package to ensure that part-time employees working ten hours or more per week have access to benefits. These initiatives demonstrate a long-term commitment to employee well-being.

Empowering Tractor Supply's team to make decisions on the front lines fosters accountability. Under Hal's guidance, the company doesn't just weather the pandemic—it also thrives. Revenues soar from $9 billion to $14.6 billion in four years. Reflecting on the journey through disruption and the inevitable challenge of the unknown, Hal says, "You don't need to have the full picture. We knew it was going to be a strong tree with deep roots and branches. I didn't know exactly what it would look like, but I knew it would have value."

Disruption You Thrust upon Yourself: Ingram Content Group's Bold Move

John Ingram stands at a 1995 book industry event in New York City, captivated by a new technology—a Xerox machine that can print books on demand. In that moment, he sees a solution to a problem that has plagued his company, the Ingram Content Group (ICG), for years: how to manage unpredictable demand for niche, low-volume titles. This isn't just a technological marvel; it could also redefine the company's future.

Founded in the late 1960s as a textbook distributor, ICG grew into the world's largest book wholesaler by the 1990s, supplying physical and digital infrastructure to the publishing industry. But forecasting demand for the "long tail" of books that may sell unpredictably over time has always been challenging. Enter print-on-demand (POD), a revolutionary technology that allows books to be printed as orders come in, eliminating the risk of accumulating unsold stock and large inventory stockpiles.

Embracing POD alters ICG's business model. Traditional offset printing requires large print runs, tying up significant capital in inventory and warehousing costs. POD, while more expensive per unit, offers flexibility and speed, allowing ICG to print quantities as low as a single book at a time. John's vision is clear: use POD to solve the challenges of overstocking inventory and thereby reshape the economics of bookselling.

The journey to fully integrate POD isn't always smooth. Growth is slow at first, and the publishing industry is hesitant to embrace the new service. Significant investment is required to scale the system.

But John's belief in POD's potential remains steadfast. By 2012, POD is not only profitable but also a cornerstone of ICG's strategy, particularly when unanticipated shifts in demand—such as those that occurred during the COVID-19 pandemic—require quick and flexible responses. And by 2021, ICG is producing more than seventy million books annually through POD, which has become a major driver of the company's revenue and operating income.

Lessons in Organizational Disruption

We can find significant takeaways from the stories of both Tractor Supply Company and Ingram Content Group.

Both embraced the potential of technological innovation to revolutionize their industries. John Ingram saw immediately that POD technology could solve long-standing problems in the book industry, allowing for more efficient inventory management and meeting unpredictable demand for niche titles. Likewise, Tractor Supply's introduction of AI-powered earpieces transformed the customer service experience, enabling team members to provide faster, more knowledgeable assistance. These examples show that adopting the right technology can create more efficient, scalable solutions and give companies a competitive edge.

Both were willing to take calculated risks. Shifting to POD was a significant departure from traditional printing methods for ICG, just as rolling out same-day delivery and curbside pickup was for Tractor Supply. Ingram invested in a technology that required substantial initial costs and had uncertain industry acceptance, and Tractor Supply invested in rapid operational changes to meet new customer demand. In both cases, these calculated risks paid off, driving meaningful change and keeping the businesses ahead in competitive markets.

Both persisted in the face of challenges. ICG's journey with POD technology wasn't smooth: the initial growth was slow, and the publishing industry was hesitant to adopt the new service. Similarly, Tractor Supply faced logistical challenges in rapidly scaling delivery and pickup services during a pandemic. But both organizations stuck it out because they believed in the long-term benefits of their innovations. Such persistence despite obstacles is critical for achieving transformative results.

Both aligned innovation with customer needs. The transition to POD directly addressed a major pain point for ICG's customers—how to manage unpredictable demand for individual books. Tractor Supply's innovations were similarly driven by the evolving needs of their new customer base, many of whom were embracing rural living for the first time. By focusing on customer pain points, both companies used their innovations to strengthen their market positions.

Both invested in a long-term vision that aligned with the fire inside their companies. As leaders, Hal and Tom had the foresight to understand that their innovations would pave the way for continual improvement in how they could serve customers. Since such service was at the core of their values, these technical upgrades fueled the fire inside each organization.

Looking to Disrupt Your Organization? Here Are a Few Places to Start

What Tractor Supply and ICG show is that disruptions don't have to be obstacles to deal with—they can be catalysts for growth. By seeing disruption as an opportunity to take your company in new and exciting directions, you can attract new customers, embrace cutting-edge technologies, and differentiate yourself in a competitive market. Whether it's through leading innovation in service delivery, adopting transformative technologies, or evolving your business model, disruptions can be the spark that propels your organization forward. The key is to stay flexible, open to change, and on the alert for the opportunity to take your business to the next level.

Embrace New Technology: Invest in emerging technologies that streamline operations and create new opportunities, just as Tractor Supply and ICG did with AI and POD, respectively.

Foster a Culture of Innovation: Encourage your team to experiment, take calculated risks, and push boundaries. This drives continual improvement. Remember the sixteen behaviors of positive disrupters? All of these behaviors exist within your organization. The goal is to create an environment where people feel safe and encouraged to collaborate.

Focus on Customer Needs: Like ICG and Tractor Supply, ensure that your innovations address real customer pain points and desires, keeping your organization customer-focused.

Invest in Talent Development: Equip your people

with the skills and knowledge they need to lead through change and navigate disruption.

Build Strategic Partnerships: Collaborate with other organizations to leverage new strengths, capabilities, and opportunities for growth.

~~~~~~

Positive Disrupter Move

Do the Scary Yes

Say "yes" to the thing that makes you nervous. Growth starts with butterflies.

~~~~~~

Chapter 29
Disrupt Your Industry

Even the smallest of disruptions can change an entire industry.

Late one evening, Andy Katz-Mayfield makes a trip to a drugstore to buy razor blades—only to find them locked away in a case. *This is absurd,* he thinks. *I'm not buying diamond jewelry; I'm buying razor blades.* As he wanders around the store trying to find a sales associate to unlock the case, he notices Gillette's overwhelming brand dominance within the razor aisle. But the product feels inauthentic to him. "There was a package with a picture of a razor blade being shot into outer space. I understood they were trying to communicate futuristic technology, but it felt cold and didn't resonate with me," he says.

Paying $25 for four razor cartridges also leaves Andy

feeling duped. "While $25 isn't a ton of money, feeling taken advantage of is a viscerally negative emotion. There wasn't any alternative unless you wanted cheap disposables, and I care about quality. I'm literally taking a blade to my face, but I'm not happy about it. I don't like the brand, the experience, or the pricing," he says in exasperation.

Andy reaches out to his friend Jeff Raider, cofounder of the eyewear brand Warby Parker. Warby Parker had recently revolutionized the eyeglasses market by offering stylish options starting at $95 — a stark contrast to the hundreds of dollars people were accustomed to spending — and their innovative business model includes allowing customers to try on frames in their own homes as well as giving away one pair of glasses for every pair sold, resulting in millions of glasses being distributed to people in need. "I had the Warby Parker model in mind. I called Jeff the next day and said, 'I think there's an opportunity in men's shaving and grooming more broadly. Can we leverage what you've learned at Warby?' And that was the origin story," Andy recounts.

Jeff, intrigued by the idea, joins Andy in exploring the shaving industry. They discover that although Gillette holds a 70 percent market share and enjoys incredible profit margins, customers share a dissatisfaction with the status quo. "When I described my experience, many guys said, 'I've had that exact experience. I know the emotion you're talking about.' That validation showed there was a real pain point," Andy says.

In 2012, Andy and Jeff cofound a new company they call Harry's. "We started as friends and remain friends. In business, you sometimes have to compartmentalize the friendship, but we share values and a common purpose," Andy notes. Creating a new razor brand is challenging. A few major players dominate the industry, and finding the right manufacturing partner is crucial. "The challenge was sourcing, manufacturing, and designing a product that met our quality expectations. We knew it wouldn't be hard to get people to try something new once, but they wouldn't return if the product didn't perform," Andy explains.

Jeff emphasizes the importance of customer experience and simplicity in product offerings. "When we started Harry's, I was writing the ad copy and responding directly to customer service emails. I spent a lot of time in the weeds because that's where our customers live and how we learn about what we can do to improve their daily lives," Jeff notes. "I like ideas that are simple and applicable. I spend a lot of time trying to streamline things with my team," he says. This approach was evident when they launched Harry's with a lineup of high-quality and user-friendly shaving essentials.

Even as Harry's expands, Jeff remains committed to understanding and serving customers. "Being at

Harry's for ten years has taught me a lot about our customers and I'm always working to deepen my understanding of the accumulated insights we have," Jeff says. He emphasizes team engagement, customer satisfaction, and financial performance as key metrics for success. And philanthropy—Harry's dedicates 1 percent of all its sales to promoting the underserved area of men's mental health, donating more than $12 million and helping two million men.

Jeff's aversion to rules, and his innovative mindset, play a significant role in Harry's market approach. "I've never seen a rule and haven't thought, 'I could break that,'" Jeff remarks. This mindset leads to non-traditional decisions, such as opting out of blister packaging when the brand launches at Target.

Harry's success has disrupted the shaving industry and resulted in a company valued at nearly $2 billion, a testament to the company's impact and innovation. "We've given consumers a choice, which is disruptive. Gillette and other competitors have had to become more consumer-oriented," Jeff explains.

Andy and Jeff's journey with Harry's proves that disruption, driven by a commitment to fairness, quality, and consumer choice, can lead to an "aha" moment that can transform an industry. Their story demonstrates the power of questioning the status quo and creating meaningful change.

Lessons from Harry's

Andy and Jeff's journey shows the challenges of shaking up a big industry. Competing against a giant such as Gillette meant they had to offer something unique. They invested heavily in marketing and used creative strategies to get noticed. Jeff even wrote the first ads himself to make the brand feel personal and genuine.

Purchasing a razor factory in Germany ensured that their blades were top-notch. They worked to showcase the better shaving experience that Harry's offers customers at a fair price. Their goal was to build a simple, high-quality, and customer-focused brand.

Securing funding allowed them to build their website, hire a team, and market their products. Ensuring that their products met legal requirements involved a lot of behind-the-scenes work. Persuading people to switch from their usual brands required demonstrating that Harry's was a better alternative.

As Harry's grew, Andy and Jeff had to maintain quality and service. Investing in research and development kept them ahead of their competitors. They adapted to economic changes so that they could continue growing. Despite such challenges, their fire inside led them to maintain focus on quality, authenticity, and high-quality customer experiences, which in turn drove their success.

Looking to Disrupt Your Industry? Here Are a Few Places to Start

Andy and Jeff's story is a powerful example of how relatively small disruptive moments can lead to breakthroughs and industry transformation. By addressing real problems, creating a trustworthy brand, and continually improving, they built a successful organization and made a significant impact on their industry.

Identify Pain Points: Look for inefficiencies or frustrations in your industry. What's your company's equivalent of overpriced razor blades locked in a drugstore case?

Partner Wisely: Collaborate with individuals whose skills and experiences are complementary to yours. Who might want to help you with production, marketing, finance, or other key functions?

Stay Customer-Focused: Understand your customers profoundly and build solutions that improve their lives. Andy and Jeff used their personal experiences as consumers to guide their decisions.

Simplify Your Approach: Start with straightforward offerings that are easy for customers to understand and use. Harry's would have struggled had it tried to launch too many kinds of shaving products right off the bat.

Challenge the Norms: Don't be afraid to question and break industry rules as you create innovative solutions. For instance, Andy and Jeff broke away from the industry trend of using plastic blister packs.

It's also a powerful story of relationships that reinforces the central message of this book. As Andy told us, "Jeff and I have known each other for twenty-plus years. Met as college interns and worked together out of college across multiple jobs and companies. Our partnership has worked because we've known each other and been friends forever—and have a deep sense of trust and shared values."

Jeff echoed the importance of relationships even in disrupting a multibillion-dollar industry. He told us, "I think about positive energy in multiple circles—family, friends, and the team at Harry's. I want my interactions to be positive and push people to get better."

Positive Disrupter Move

Check Your Daily Habits

The way you're doing things—Good? Bad? Somewhere in between? If it's not good, tweak it or toss it.

Quick Recap: Achieve

Achieving success and making a positive impact begins with disrupting yourself and extends to various areas of life.

Your Relationships: Strengthen and transform the connections you have with other people, fostering mutual growth and support.

Your Family: Create a nurturing and dynamic environment that encourages all members to thrive and pursue their passions.

Your Team: Lead and inspire by embracing innovative approaches and achieving collective goals.

Your Organization: Drive change by fostering a culture of disruption that encourages continual improvement and adaptation.

Your Industry: Influence and revolutionize by setting new standards and pioneering advancements that benefit society as a whole.

Although disruption can show up in various places,

there is no one path you must take. You might disrupt yourself and then change an industry or you might disrupt yourself and then focus on disrupting a personal relationship or your family situation. It's your life; you're in charge.

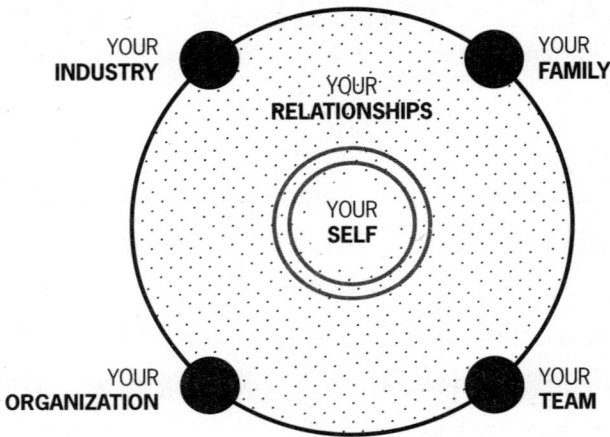

Disrupting Beyond Yourself: Scaling from 1 to 1,000 and Beyond

Disruption always starts with you. You can't shake up the world around you until you've shaken up yourself. Once you decide to make big changes that impact hundreds, thousands, or even more, you still always begin with one person: yourself.

As you look to disrupt your relationships, family, team, organization, industry, and beyond, it's important to know how to scale disruption—to take it from one person to five, to ten, to a hundred, to a thousand, and beyond. Here are five Cs you'll want to lean on:

- **Clarity.** First, get clear on your purpose. Just like you've uncovered the fire inside yourself, you need to figure out the purpose behind whatever it is you're looking to disrupt. Being crystal clear on your "why" and your goals is what makes it possible to take the right actions when things get messy.

- **Communication.** Disruption never happens in a vacuum. If you want to move people toward change — or even just keep things steady — you've got to communicate where you're headed and why it matters. And just as important, you need to create space for others to share their thoughts, too. Disrupting beyond yourself is a two-way conversation.

- **Collaboration.** No one disrupts at scale alone. Pull together the talents, strengths, and ideas of the people around you to collaborate on something bigger and better than you could on your own. Get them involved early and give them a sense of ownership. When it's their journey, too, they're far more likely to stick with it.

- **Commitment.** Being committed to your vision is critical—especially when the going gets tough…which it probably will! That's when you will need to be most fully committed to clarity, communication, and collaboration.
- **Consistency.** Finally, stick with it. Be steady. Stay on message. Don't let every obstacle knock you off course. Consistency builds trust, and trust keeps the momentum alive.

As you go forward, keep these ideas in mind. Scaling disruption isn't just about shaking things up—it's about making a lasting impact, and you can't do that without clarity, communication, collaboration, commitment, and consistency.

And remember, just as you've uncovered the fire inside yourself, take the time to explore the fire inside your relationships, family, team, and beyond. When you're clear on what really matters, it's so much easier to see how disruption can bring you closer to—or further from—your mission.

To get started, turn to Part VII: Your Positive Disrupter Toolkit (p.301) and Tool 2: Craft Your Mission Statement (p.313). Big changes might start small, but with the right approach, they can ripple outward and transform everything around you.

Part VI
Refine

Chapter 30

It Takes a Posse

Get key players involved at every level.

In her early twenties, Debbie Bial is working with youth in New York City when she notices a troubling trend: bright, talented students from diverse backgrounds are dropping out of college. "They were going off to college, and we noticed that many of them were coming home, dropping out. It made no sense because we knew them personally. We knew they were smart, talented, and capable," she recalls.

A simple remark from one student sparks a solution: "I never would have dropped out of college if I'd had my posse with me." This statement stops Debbie in her tracks and ignites a brilliant idea: *Why not have a posse or a team of kids go to college together?*

This moment leads to the creation of the Posse

Foundation, a merit-based program, which sends students to college in supportive groups of between ten and twelve peers. Debbie finds the start-up assistance she needs in Terry Deal, then a distinguished professor at Vanderbilt University's Peabody College and a specialist in organizational behavior and development work.

"He loved the idea and helped get the players involved," Debbie recounts. Vanderbilt takes a chance on the first Posse class, recognizing the potential in these students despite SAT scores that fall below Vanderbilt norms.

Over the years, Posse cohorts have thrived, silencing critics and proving the validity of a new disruptive model for college admissions based on finding public high school students with extraordinary academic and leadership potential who might have been overlooked by traditional college-selection processes. Today, Posse's partner colleges and universities award Posse scholars full-tuition leadership scholarships.

But it was not always that way.

When the foundation begins, Posse needs to raise 20 percent of scholarship funding itself. Five years in, Debbie and Terry are having trouble doing so. Fortunately, Michael Ainslie, then the CEO of Sotheby's and a member of Vanderbilt's Board of Trust, steps in to help find a solution. "Posse intrigued me because this program offered an elite college opportunity to a new cadre of deserving students. It was fundamentally challenging for kids to get admitted to college. We needed to disrupt the old model," he says.

Michael brings Debbie to a restaurant near Lincoln Center, where he lays out a plan. "Let's create a new 501(c)(3), the Posse Foundation. You be the executive director, and I will become the chairman of the board, and we will create a board in the next few weeks." Debbie agrees.

"By the time we met Michael, we knew the program worked," she recounts, "but we had a financial model that wasn't sustainable. We were building up a debt to our university partner. Michael offered a disruptive idea. He believed that we were finding such outstanding students that the university partner would fund all of the scholarships and then proceeded to convince Vanderbilt's chancellor of this new approach."

At the end of 2023, the Posse Foundation has net assets approaching $150 million.

In 2021, the foundation evolves when Lin-Manuel Miranda partners with Posse to create the Posse Arts and Posse Puerto Rico programs. Posse is now sending scholars to five new university partners, including the California Institute of the Arts and the University of North Carolina School of the Arts.

Doug Christiansen, Vanderbilt vice provost for university enrollment and dean of admissions and financial aid, points out that "Vanderbilt would not be the institution it is today without Posse. Since 1989, the program has helped us think differently about who needs to be in a classroom to make it more educationally dynamic and sound. It is a collaboration that, after thirty-five years, continues to yield incredible results."

One such result is Dr. Shirley M. Collado, part of that first Vanderbilt Posse. At age fifteen, Shirley meets Debbie through the CityKids Foundation in New York City, and a few years later, Debbie asks her, "Have you ever thought about going away to college?" Initially, Shirley thinks it's impossible—her family relies on her too much. But a pivotal endorsement changes everything: Her maternal grandmother tells Shirley's father, "God is giving you this as a gift that none of us could ever give your daughter, and she's earned it, so let her go." With her family's blessing, Shirley embarks on the first Posse journey.

Dr. Shirley M. Collado graduates from Vanderbilt with honors and earns her PhD at Duke. She has completed ten years on the Vanderbilt Board of Trust and is the first woman of color to be voted in as trustee emerita at VU, the first woman of color to serve as an officer of the Board of Trust at VU, and the first Posse scholar to serve on a university or college board of trustees. She becomes the ninth president of Ithaca College and the first person of color to lead the institution — and the first Dominican American to ever lead a four-year college or university in the United States. She then partners with Laurene Powell Jobs, the founder and board chair of College Track, and becomes president and CEO of College Track.

Monique Nelson-Nwachuku is another Posse scholar. Today, she serves as the CEO of UniWorld Group, a leading multicultural marketing agency. Like Shirley Collado, she is one of thousands of Posse scholars who earned the chance to participate in the program and used it to change herself and others.

Juan Rajlin, vice president and treasurer of Alphabet and Google and a member of Posse's National Board, puts it this way: "I grew up in Argentina and came to the US to go to school. So access to education quite literally changed the trajectory of my life. Posse's mission — to give access to college to kids with extraordinary leadership ability who might be overlooked — is personal to me, as it is to many others who sit on the board. We all share a true passion for the mission of Posse."

Debbie Bial's vision and dedication showcase the transformative power of community and mutual support as well as a commitment to continual refinement and improvement—resulting in an organization that disrupts itself in order to grow stronger and better than ever before. An ability and willingness to review achievements, reflect on them, revise approaches, and recommit to improvement is called the Refine step of the Positive Disrupter Loop.

The Refine Model

Many people skip this crucial Refine step after achieving a degree of success, but doing so can hinder long-term progress.

Two retired army four-star generals, Stanley McChrystal and David Petraeus, have emphasized the importance of the Refine step during discussions. Petraeus put it this way: "We used to say that after a particular operation or training event...the more you beat yourself up, the more open you are about what you didn't get right—the more you're going to learn from it." But don't "beat yourself up" too badly, as long as you learn and improve. Consider Debbie's story, full of refinement efforts—she realized the financial model wouldn't work and, with Michael's help, found a new way forward.

Review: Look at the results. Debbie initially identified a problem with the Posse Foundation's financial model and saw the need for a sustainable solution.

Reflect: Consider progress and impact. Debbie was willing to listen and learn from Michael so she could understand the broader implications of the financial model.

Revise: Adjust the approach. Debbie and Michael revised the funding approach to ensure sustainability, which involved creating a new foundation and building a dedicated board.

Recommit: Commit to getting better. Debbie's continual commitment to improving the program led to its significant growth and expanded reach.

The Posse Foundation's disruptive efforts tie in to the overarching theme of relationships and family. All relationships form, change, and deepen—including those between Michael and Debbie, among Posse scholars, and between Debbie and everyone who's gone through the program. Beyond the scholars themselves, the powerful impact of positive disruption can be felt through countless families and generations touched by Posse. The program has transformed individual lives and strengthened family bonds, creating generational change through education and opportunity.

Positive Disrupter Move

Put It on the Table

If the vibe's off, say, "Let's be real. Here's what I'm sensing."

Chapter 31
Overcoming Resistance to Disruption

Dare to suck.

After graduating from college, a young country music fan named Jim Beavers goes looking for work in Nashville, the Country Music Capital of the World. He's happy to take a job in the mail room at Capitol Records, hoping he can work his way up on the business side of the music industry. With a long-term goal of running a record company someday, he studies part-time for his MBA and joins the finance department.

Jim never considers a career in songwriting, even though he's a passionate amateur musician. But the longer he works on the business side, the more he feels himself getting pulled over to the creative side.

"I would go home from my finance job and write

songs," he recalls. "I never put two and two together. Maybe I didn't have the confidence to pursue it."

Jim knows that all songwriters face overwhelming odds. Most of their output will likely never be heard, never generate income, never change anyone's life. Daring to create new songs inevitably means failing a lot and being rejected a lot. Jim has no interest in facing that kind of constant resistance.

But after about ten years, he experiences a layoff. At first he's crushed with disappointment. But then Jim leans into the disruption and listens to the inner voice that's been urging him toward songwriting. He uses his severance as a financial cushion to give it a shot. At this point he knows the music business and the market for songs. He also has a lot of friends who are writers. So it's not a crazy risk — it's a calculated risk.

That layoff, he recalls twenty years later, "ended up being the best thing that ever happened to me." But only because Jim overcame his fear of rejection.

"I've probably written a thousand songs, and only twenty of those songs are hits. There are people who have written a thousand who have *never* had a hit." Jim is like a farmer who throws out a thousand seeds but cannot predict which ones are going to sprout. All he can do is keep farming.

Sometimes, he explains, writing a song is like solving a math problem. You keep playing with various ideas for the chords, the melody, the lyrics, the title. If it doesn't all fit together, you either keep grinding away or give up on it. But if you're lucky, the full answer eventually hits you as if it were obvious all along.

As Jim notes, "A lot of people aren't used to being uncomfortable, if they are used to controlling their environment and controlling outcomes." To make it as a professional songwriter, he had to become "very comfortable with being uncomfortable all the time. I have to dare to suck."

Jim comes to accept that he might work hard on a song he loves that will never earn a dime or please a single listener. "You cannot get emotionally invested in a song, or it'll drive you nuts. I focus only on what I can control. I control my effort and attitude. I control how hard I work and how I respond to whatever happens." But he can't control how other people react to his music.

This attitude drives the writing of a song he calls "Red Solo Cup." Inspired by the college football fans he sees drinking out of red cups at a tailgate, he plays with some goofy lyrics about drinking with friends. But is the song *too* goofy? Will people laugh at it instead of with it? Jim forges ahead despite his doubts, and despite the skepticism of his writing partners.

Country superstar Toby Keith ends up recording "Red Solo Cup"—and it becomes a big crossover hit on both the country and pop charts.

As Jim concludes, "I've learned if you really believe an idea is good, you've got to keep going and get around the wall."

Resistance Is the Leading Enemy of Disruption

No matter how good your disruptive idea is, you will need to get other people on board with it. But many people are deeply resistant to change, whether out of anxiety, past bad experiences, force of habit, superstition, or simple laziness. In any area of life that requires the support of others, you may hear pushback such as...

We tried that once before and it failed.
That's not how we do things here.
This idea is too weird to succeed.
Why can't we just stick with what works?

Tina Seelig, an expert on the creative process, describes brainstorming as both an art *and* a science. In a supportive, collaborative environment, everyone can be creative in their own way. The best leaders dare to say, *"This is a wild and crazy idea. It's gonna either soar or crash."*

So instead of trying to squash someone else's idea with *"Are you nuts? That'll never work,"* try a more encouraging response. Something like *"Well, that's interesting and different. Let's build on it together and see how we might make it work."*

If you're the boss, you might be able to order your team members to adopt your disruptive new ideas. But in many workplace situations—and even more often in family and social situations—you may not have the authority (or desire) to simply say, "My way or the highway!" Besides, winning voluntary commitment rather than enforcing resentful compliance is always more effective.

Show them that you're serious about solving the problem. If you have a history of making halfhearted changes but not following through, people may assume that this change won't last, either. So they may try to wait you out.

You may need to persuade others to at least *try* new ways of doing things before passing judgment on them. You may also need to inspire them to start doing more work than usual, or different kinds of work that are unfamiliar.

Not easy!

Family: Rebalancing the Mental Load

Corinne, a forty-seven-year-old mom, carries what's known as the "mental load" of her family. As the

269

unofficial scheduling coordinator for two working parents and three kids attending three different schools, she was at her wit's end.

The kids alone—a fifteen-year-old boy, a thirteen-year-old girl, and an eleven-year-old boy—all had jam-packed after-school and weekend schedules, including sports practices, dance classes, piano lessons, playdates, birthday parties, and on and on.

Someone had to keep track of who needed to be where at any given moment and with which supplies, plus figure out the logistics for all those pickups and drop-offs. And on top of making sure everyone got from point A to point B on time, there was a dog who needed to be fed and walked twice a day...the kids' appointments for doctors and dentists...all the school forms and activity registrations to be filled out and paid for...birthday presents for their friends' parties to be bought and wrapped...and much more.

That someone, inevitably, was Corinne. She had begged her family repeatedly to help her manage it. But over and over, despite her husband and kids' promises to help, the old pattern of Mom handling all the logistics always returned. Corinne was desperate to disrupt this overwhelming situation and get back to the family's deeper purpose and values: everyone respecting one another and working together for the greater good.

A friend told her about a collaborative calendar app

that could be updated by everyone in the family from their phones or laptops, enabling them to share their plans as soon as they developed and make changes in real time. The app was easy to use, even for the youngest kid.

Corinne was excited as she started uploading *everything* to this shared calendar, including whose turn it was to feed and walk the dog each day. Everyone agreed to start using it to make organizing and planning easier.

Problem solved? Not so fast.

At first her husband and kids did use the calendar. But within only a few days, their old habits kicked back in. They neglected to update their individual events and stopped trying to work around other people's needs.

For instance, on Tuesday night, the fifteen-year-old said, "Hey, Mom, my soccer practice moved to Wednesday this week. Can you take me?" Problem was, his practice now clashed with his sister's dance class on the other side of town — and he neglected to mention that he'd been notified about the change a week earlier.

Two days later, the husband had a work event he'd forgotten to put on the calendar, which would keep him away from home much later than usual. He didn't even remember that it was supposed to be his turn to drive a carpool and walk the dog.

Even the thirteen-year-old, usually Corinne's most cooperative child, never mentioned or uploaded the invitation to the party she was supposed to attend that coming weekend.

Of course Corinne's loved ones weren't intentionally sabotaging her attempts to share the mental load. They weren't motivated by hostility or aggression. Still, they were resisting her attempt at disruption, and they didn't seem all that invested in changing their habits. If Corinne wanted to overcome this resistance, she would have to act decisively and quickly. But how?

Tactics for Overcoming Resistance to Disruption

Stress the seriousness of the problem. Others may not grasp the scope of the issues if they're only visible from your perspective.

Envision a positive future. "Imagine" is a powerful word—use it to help people begin to think about what's possible. Focusing on a better tomorrow can have a bigger impact than focusing on today's challenges.

Invite contributions to a solution. Remember this principle: "No involvement = no commitment." When people have the chance to add their fingerprints, they are more likely to take ownership of the solutions and work to make them stick.

Listen to objections with an open mind. Maybe a team-mate or family member has a valid reason for not supporting your disruptive idea. It's possible that you haven't considered every potential downside. Make it clear that you want their honest feedback, then modify your idea if appropriate.

If you get verbal agreement but no action, probe deeper. Often the stated reason for resistance isn't the real reason. For instance, people may be reluctant to admit that they simply don't want to change a comfortable routine or take on extra work. Or maybe they don't even agree that the problem is actually a problem. Or maybe they want to change but don't know how — they may lack the skill but not the will. You can't overcome resistance if you don't understand it!

Hang in there. Some changes need to be implemented gradually if you want them to stick. You might be dealing with people who will respond to modest changes made one at a time rather than a complete process overhaul.

Corinne's Response to Resistance

Corinne called a family meeting after that first, failed attempt with the new scheduling app.

First, she calmly explained the urgency of the problem, this time with more detail. Their old way of life was making her increasingly anxious and unhappy, and they all knew that her bad moods would make things unpleasant for everyone else. So it was in everyone's best interest to help solve the problem.

Corinne also stressed that she was deadly serious about rebalancing the family's mental load. She wasn't going to give up on the shared calendar, and she wasn't going to tolerate others who gave up. So they could either invest the time in making it a new habit, or they could listen to her daily reminders.

She asked for objections and listened carefully. When the fifteen-year-old pointed out that kids can't control the timing of sports practices or games, she agreed that no one should ever get in trouble for schedule changes beyond their control. They would only be expected to flag schedule conflicts as soon as they found out about them, in order to give the family time to adjust.

Finally, she promised to reward everyone with a dinner out at the family's favorite restaurant if they all stuck with the new plan for the following week. And sure enough, they all used it faithfully in week two.

In the days and months that followed, there were still some occasional glitches and forgotten updates, but the value in having a complete and current shared calendar was quickly evident to everyone. And before too long, this disruption became the family's new way of life.

Business: Changing the Formula

Steve was the marketing director for a division of a huge global book publisher (known as an "imprint" in publishing lingo). Three times a year, he was responsible for preparing PowerPoint slides for their seasonal sales conference, during which each imprint would present its upcoming books to the company's 100-plus sales reps and senior executives. Sometimes these conferences took place in person; other times they were done remotely. Either way, Steve felt pressure to make his imprint's fifty-minute time slot as impactful as possible.

As far back as anyone could remember, the slides for these presentations had followed a strict formula. Every upcoming book was showcased the same way: An image of its cover, a headshot of the author, and bullet points detailing the book's subject and marketing plan, plus a list of the author's previous books.

Steve had always found this formula boring — especially the parade of similar bullet points for book after book. Each season, Steve could *feel* the audience fighting to stay awake. He knew that the enthusiasm of the sales force was essential to the success of their books, so he felt desperate to make his next presentation more exciting.

Without asking anyone's permission, Steve decided to disrupt the process. He drafted a very different slide show, one he felt was more entertaining. Instead of standard author headshots, he asked the authors to submit candid pictures—at home with their families or pets, or while practicing their favorite hobbies. Soon the PowerPoint was filled with cute dogs and cats and authors playing guitar or crocheting.

Instead of an endless sea of bullet points, he interspersed the presentation with short homemade video clips, so the authors themselves could share why they were excited about their upcoming books and what kind of readers would find them appealing.

Steve also asked a graphic designer on his team to spice up the slides with bolder colors and more distinctive fonts. He was thrilled when he saw how her changes made the key points pop off the screen.

He imagined their presentation becoming the talk of the entire conference and couldn't wait to show it to his boss, the head of their imprint. Unfortunately, his boss didn't share Steve's excitement. On the contrary, she was horrified. "That's not the way we do things! Are you trying to get us all in trouble?" She told him to go back and redo it the standard way.

In the face of this resistance, Steve could have given up. Instead, he applied some of the same tactics that worked for Corinne:

He made a calm case to his boss that increasing enthusiasm at the conference could deliver a real boost to their bottom line, and spicing up the presentation was a great way to drive that enthusiasm.

He noted that even if they got pushback from some traditionalists, it would also spark conversations about how their imprint was forward-thinking and bold. How could that be bad?

He took his boss's objections seriously — especially her concern that some of the authors looked foolish in their homemade pictures and videos, and it would be bad if the audience started laughing. Steve agreed to restore a few traditional headshots and replace several video clips with more traditional bullets, while keeping the overall new format and design.

He nudged his boss to admit that she was worried about how her own boss — their notoriously strict division president — would react. Steve promised to take any heat that might come from above and would not deflect responsibility onto anyone else.

After some further modifications, they gave the disruptive presentation at sales conference and got enthusiastic responses — including from Steve's boss's boss.

As you begin to embrace disruption in both your work life and your personal life, don't let resistance bring you down. As Jim Beavers says, you've got to keep going and find a way around whatever walls people put in your path. Most (though not all) walls usually can be surmounted with some persistence and smart tactics. And in the meantime, "dare to suck."

Positive Disrupter Move

Break Your Everyday Pattern

Change your route. Your lunch. Your playlist. Small switch, fresh brain.

Chapter 32
Leading Through Disruption

It's always possible to win over skeptics and find allies.

At age twenty, unsure about his future, Vincent Stanley joins his uncle's small business, which mostly produces and sells gear for mountain climbing. He's not an outdoorsman, but Vincent is drawn to the company's culture. "It was collegial, not authoritarian," he recalls. "I liked the climbers and surfers and the love they had for the natural world."

His daring uncle, Yvon Chouinard, actually *is* an outdoorsman. He has scaled the granite cliff faces of Yosemite National Park using climbing spikes called pitons, which he forged by hand from a harvester blade to provide stability when hammered into cracks in the rock.

By the early 1970s, the company has a reputation for

producing excellent gear, including pitons made from chrome-molybdenum steel that climbers consider essential.

Then it's discovered that those pitons, their biggest-selling product, are damaging mountains. Now they face a moral dilemma. Unwilling to perpetuate environmental disfigurement, Yvon pivots his company to invent "clean climbing," which challenges climbers to scale heights without damaging nature.

They switch to selling reusable aluminum tools called chocks and hexes that won't alter the rock. And they announce the shift in their catalog via an unusual twelve-page article that's part environmental manifesto, part equipment instruction guide.

"Within nine months," Vincent says, "it changed the way Americans climb. That article was discussed in every climbing magazine as the basis of every route. And within nine months our business had changed from 70 percent pitons to 70 percent chocks."

This will hardly be the last time the company—relaunched as Patagonia and expanding into many new product lines—will lead a disruption that spreads across its industry. Time and again, Yvon will prioritize core values of sustainability and protecting the planet. He'd rather risk losing money, or even risk losing his whole company, than betray his environmental values and set a bad example.

For instance, in the 1990s Patagonia learns that the cotton it uses to make clothing, which they've always viewed as a benign natural fiber, is actually produced with intensive chemicals. They decide to change suppliers, ditching environmentally unfriendly standard cotton for more expensive organic cotton.

This is such a disruptive idea that even Patagonia employees, whose values typically align with the company's, protest this proposed shift. The downsides are clear:

It will require building entirely new supplier relationships.

It will require creating entirely new production logistics and processes.

It will require raising prices across the board to pay for it.

Why are we taking an action that not a single customer has asked for? many ask.

As Vincent puts it, "We had a small revolt on our hands. Though a gentle one, because it was Patagonia."

The reasons behind the decision become clear through practical demonstration. Field trips to a non-organic Central Valley cotton farm deliver an unnerving sensory experience.

As Vincent recalls, "The minute the buses got to the cotton fields, you could smell the [unpleasant] chemicals, because the organophosphates used as fertilizer were originally developed as a nerve gas during World War I. And if you put your hands in the soil, there was no life in it, no vegetation, no worms. People would come back and say, 'What we're doing is a royal pain, but the company's doing the right thing, and I'm going to help make it work.'"

This pivotal moment sets the stage for many future Patagonia disruptions in how clothing and outdoor gear can be produced, marketed, and recycled sustainably. Such disruptions have made it one of the world's most admired companies, as well as a consistently growing and profitable one. As Yvon once told an interviewer, "I know it sounds crazy, but every time I have made a decision that's best for the planet, I've made money."

Even in his mid-eighties, a time of life when most leaders are either retired or stuck in the past, Yvon is still innovating and disrupting. In 2022 he announces that his family will donate 98 percent of the company's equity to an environmental nonprofit. "Instead of extracting value from nature and transforming it into wealth, we are using the wealth Patagonia creates to protect the source. We're making Earth our only shareholder. I am dead serious about saving this planet."

Like his uncle's, Vincent's fire inside after all these years is Patagonia's environmental work. "To me, this is the best use of business as a force in society," he says proudly. "We're looking at problems that we have as a society and as a planet, and introducing something that creates change that couldn't create change before."

Disruption Without Purpose Is Just Noise

People are more likely to embrace disruption when they understand why it matters and how it moves the mission forward. Patagonia's inspiring history of leading through disruption offers some powerful principles that can also apply to leading a family, a club, a church group, or any other kind of organization. For instance . . .

Showing Often Beats Telling

Upon learning that carefully considered products were hurting the planet, any environmentalist might become demoralized, even paralyzed. Not Yvon Chouinard.

He could have kept trying to convince his resistant employees of the benefits of the disruption he envisioned. But he realized that it would be far more effective to *show* people the reality of nonorganic cotton fields, where all those chemicals made the air stink and the soil feel lifeless.

Instead of giving up in frustration, Patagonia immediately turned challenges into positive opportunities, finding ways to disrupt the status quo while realigning their practices with their purpose and core values. In the process, they modeled a healthy approach to disruption for the core team — and an entire industry.

Whether it's an unexpected change at work, a challenge in your family, or any curveball life throws your way, the key isn't just surviving but using these moments to fuel the fire inside yourself, your team, and your family.

A positive disrupter redefines problems as opportunities to rethink tasks on the way to creating solutions that are often new and untested. These behaviors refine the cycle of the Positive Disrupter Loop.

Disruptions Often Lead to Growth

Change feels uncomfortable, but it's also where the biggest breakthroughs happen. That's why, at work, it's important to remind people of prior times when disruption led to success. Ask: "Remember when we thought that change was going to be tough? Look where we are now." Stress that disruption isn't the enemy — it's part of progress.

At home, reflect on past challenges that made your family stronger. "Remember when we moved, and it was hard at first? Now look at the new friendships we've built." Children are always watching how their parents and family members handle change and uncertainty. If you focus on possible solutions instead of your anxiety, they'll learn how to do the same. Connect the dots so disruption is seen as a stepping stone, not a setback.

Fight the Urge to Default to "Let's Do What We've Always Done"

As we've seen, whenever uncertainty hits, people tend to cling to the familiar — even if the familiar no longer serves them. A useful question in these situations: "Is this really the best way, or is it just the way we've always done it?" Challenge automatic thinking.

At work, ask, "If we were building this from scratch today, would we still do it this way?" If the answer is no, it's time for a rethink.

At home, reconsider habits that don't work anymore. Maybe dinner routines need a refresh, weekend activities need a shake-up, or certain traditions aren't serving the family anymore.

Tie Every Change to Purpose — Make the "Why" Clear

People are more likely to embrace disruption when they understand why it's happening and why it matters.

At work, don't just announce a change; connect it to how it moves the mission forward. How does it better serve your organization's values and fire inside? Instead of saying, "We're shifting this process," say, "We're making this shift because it will help us serve our customers better and make your job easier." Give people a reason to care.

At home, if you need to announce a disappointing change to your family, ground the conversation in shared values. Whenever you face tough decisions like taking on new responsibilities due to the birth of a new child or the illness of an older family member, remind everyone in the family of the bigger why. "I know this feels hard, but our new roles will help us grow closer as a family and open up new opportunities."

Make Space for Shared Ownership

People resist whatever they feel is being forced on them. The best way to get buy-in—or, better yet, people's best ideas and efforts—is to let them help navigate the ship.

At work, encourage brainstorming to question out-dated processes and explore new ideas. You might even call the meetings "disruption sessions."

Ask: "If we were starting from scratch today, how would we do this differently?" Instead of rolling out change from the top down, involve your team in shaping the way forward. Don't be surprised when their suggestions are better than anything you could dream up on your own.

Ask: "What's the best way we can make this work?"

Don't forget to start with the first step. Small, visible changes build momentum.

At home, instead of making unilateral decisions, bring the whole family into problem-solving. Instead of "We're doing this," say, "This is happening—how do we want to handle it together?" Or: "What's another way we might handle this?" Or: "If we could reinvent how we do X from scratch, what might that look like?"

Shared ownership turns resistance into momentum.

Cross-Pollinate Ideas—Mix up Who's in the Conversation

The best ideas come from unexpected places and the interaction of different perspectives.

At work, get people from different teams or backgrounds into the same room. When different skill sets mix, fresh solutions emerge—so encourage your team to collaborate by seeking out insights beyond their usual circle.

At home, expose your family to new ways of thinking. Travel, read, meet new people, or just mix up routines. If you want different results, bring in different perspectives. You never know who might have an out-of-the-box insight.

Push for Progress, Not Perfection

Fear of failure often stops people from pursuing disruptive actions. But you can overcome that fear by starting with small wins to build momentum. Instead of changing everything all at once, try some simple experiments in the direction of your long-term goals.

At work, shift the mindset from "we have to get this right" to "let's test this out and see what we learn." Quick experiments can sometimes lead to big breakthroughs. And instead of treating any setback as a catastrophe, focus on your team's growth via testing and learning. You can always adjust later if those experiments don't quite work. Make it clear that trying, learning, and adjusting is better than standing still.

At home, normalize learning through mistakes. Ask, "What's something new you tried this week? What did you learn?" Instead of making failure a big deal, make growth the focus.

Leading Through the Generational Shift

"It's very difficult to shift a culture without support from the top," Vincent Stanley observes. "But at the same time, you can have support from the top and fail to shift a culture because it doesn't go very deep."

Leaders of all experience levels will find that people often resist change, he adds, "not so much because it's operationally difficult but because it challenges the imagination. And if they don't have the experience of doing business a certain way, they don't have the confidence. So what you want to do is raise the confidence level in the organization."

A strong leader isn't threatened by bold new ideas from younger colleagues. They recognize that a fresh perspective might be exactly what's needed. Of course novices will be wrong sometimes — experience really *is* valuable — but that doesn't mean their insights should be dismissed. Instead of brushing new concepts aside, good leaders ask questions, listen, and learn.

You might be surprised by what newcomers who aren't weighed down by conventional wisdom can contribute.

On the flip side, if, as a young person, you find yourself in a company where not a lot of people align with your ideas, start by finding your allies. Figure out a couple of simple changes that nobody can quarrel with. When those are successful, try others that are more ambitious. This path will usually, gradually, bring more people over to your side. But if it doesn't, you can find another company that you want to work for more.

Ask yourself a few essential questions:

What are your values? What do you care about most?
What is your strongest source of satisfaction?
How are you useful to others? What do people call on you for?

"A lot of work is chores," says Vincent, "so do something that brings something back to you. Maybe not at the end of the first day, but after two or three years you can look back and say, oh my gosh, I can't believe that we actually did that. That makes a difference to me and I'm going to build on that for my life."

It takes a little time, but it does happen.

Positive Disrupter Move

Say the Right Thing

That honest thought you keep swallowing? Say it with kindness and clarity.

Chapter 33

Go Disrupt Something

In the midst of disruption, take stock of what matters most.

The sun is setting on a seemingly perfect day at Percy Priest Lake, outside Nashville, Tennessee. Laughter and camaraderie fill the air . . . until everything changes in a split second. Luke, a college student enjoying the day with friends, makes a fateful dive from a pontoon boat, unaware of the sandbar lurking just below the surface. The impact is immediate and devastating: fractured C4 and C5 vertebrae, a life hanging in the balance, and a group of friends thrown into a whirlwind of fear and uncertainty.

Teddy Raskin, one of Luke's friends, arrives shortly after the paramedics. Even in this dire situation, Teddy is struck by his friend's optimism. Despite facing a life-threatening injury and the uncertainty of whether he will ever walk again, Luke remains remarkably calm and positive, even cracking jokes with the people around him. This unwavering spirit profoundly affects Teddy, and driven by a deep empathy for his friend and a strong desire to help, he commits to raising money for the vital medical equipment Luke will require.

Combining a passion for music with his fundraising goal, Teddy organizes a concert at their school with the ambitious goal of raising the $90,000 needed for the rehabilitation equipment that could offer Luke a chance at recovery. But the event is about more than just raising money — it's also about rallying a community in support of Luke.

Teddy names the concert Lights on the Lawn. Bringing it to life was no small feat. Teddy faced countless obstacles, from persuading people to donate, attend, and perform to managing the logistics of such a large-scale event. "I was asking for Afrojack for, like, $10,000 and Swedish House Mafia for $20,000," he says of his naivete in approaching these musical acts. "These agents were like, 'Did you leave a zero off the offer letter?'" Teddy says. Yet through creativity, determination, and deep care for others, Teddy and the team he builds not only reach their goal of successfully funding Luke's medical devices; they also establish a philanthropic legacy that extends well beyond that single performance. Over the course of the following decade, Lights on the Lawn becomes a yearly event and raises nearly $1 million, donating 100 percent of its proceeds to East Nashville's Mary Parrish Center, a charity supporting survivors of domestic violence. Its mission is summed up by its motto: "Music that matters."

Over time, Teddy's desire to help people overcome unforeseen challenges has only grown. A decade after that day by the lake, the lesson that profound positive achievements can emerge from disruption still resonates with Teddy when he watches footage of Russia's invasion of Ukraine. The need is clear: Ukraine requires medical supplies, and Teddy, now several years into running a medical supply company called KOACORE, is in a position to help.

Drawing upon the same determination that drove him to create Lights on the Lawn, Teddy acts with conscience to navigate the complexities of international aid. Partnering with WeShield and the Ukrainian Congress Committee of America, he spearheads an initiative to deliver more than $35 million worth of aid, including eighty thousand first-aid kits and 126 ambulances, directly to the front lines—embodying the very essence of positive disruption.

Teddy's journey from the shores of Percy Priest Lake to the front lines of Ukraine underscores a vital truth: Each disruption, no matter how daunting, offers a chance to throw fuel on the fire inside, to make meaningful change and push yourself closer to your good life.

Teddy's path is solely his own, shaped by his experiences, passions, and choices in response to life's challenges.

What about you? Are you living a good life?

A strong *yes* starts by clarifying the fire inside you and then using your life's disruptions to fuel your inner fire.

Consider the four foundational facts:

1. The status quo is a deceptive little devil.
2. You're wired to disrupt.
3. Relationships provide headwinds and tailwinds.
4. Your time here is finite—make it count in ways that matter.

Consider the five roles:

1. Trailblazer
2. Firefighter
3. Torchbearer
4. Fire Chief
5. Tinder Gatherer

Consider the sixteen key behaviors of a positive disrupter:

Brain		Heart	
1	Think deeply to uncover insights	9	Care about others
2	Believe better is possible	10	Act on your conscience
Eyes		Gut	
3	Have a vision	11	Trust your instincts
4	See brutal reality	12	Push past the butterflies
Ears		Hands	
5	Listen to understand	13	Let go of good to get better
6	Hear what's not said	14	Get your hands dirty
Mouth		Feet	
7	Say something smart	15	Run toward disruption
8	Stay on message	16	Stand firm despite doubters

Examine how to achieve results in various facets of life: your self, your relationships, your family, your team, your organization, and your industry. Refine your approach and continually get better.

Now it's your turn.

How will you work with these ideas and make them your own?

You don't have to travel to India, as Pia did; quit

your job to start a fashion business, as Josie did; or follow the path of anyone else profiled in this book. Those stories are about how other people found their good lives. But what are you going to do to find yours?

So what's your story going to be? How will you disrupt your status quo and create a life that fuels your fire inside? The next chapter is yours to write.

~~~~~~~~~~~~~~~~~~~~~~~~~~~~~~~~~~~~~

Positive Disrupter Move

Ask for More

Want the shot? The help? The truth? Ask for it. Closed mouths stay stuck.

~~~~~~~~~~~~~~~~~~~~~~~~~~~~~~~~~~~~~

Quick Recap: Refine

Reflect on the lessons of Refine, a crucial step to long-term progress.

1. **Review Your Achievements:** Objectively assess your results. What did your efforts achieve?
2. **Reflect on Them:** Consider the significance of your progress and impact. What do these results mean?
3. **Revise Approaches:** Adjust your strategies based on your reflections. What could you do differently in the future?
4. **Recommit to Improvement:** Determine your next steps for continued growth. What should you do next? And how will you commit to making it happen?

Disrupting Beyond Yourself

The chapters on overcoming resistance and leading through disruption are all about other people: the families, teams, and organizations that you will need to bring with you. As you reflect on them as well, focus on how essential it is to remain open to other people's ideas; to share your successes and struggles alike; to capture lessons learned with a spirit of collective learning; and to appreciate each small bit of progress you make along the way.

Think about how Debbie Bial used the transformative power of community and mutual support to drive continual refinement and improvement of her very successful nonprofit.

Think about how Jim Beavers shifted his mindset to thrive as a songwriter—a profession in which resistance and rejection are daily companions.

Think about how Corinne convinced her husband and kids to get past "how we've always done things" to adopt a fairer distribution of the family's mental load.

Think about how Steve disrupted his team's usual way of presenting at sales conference, making the process more enjoyable and effective for everyone involved.

Think about how Patagonia repeatedly disrupted its own business model as well as its entire industry, by making every decision in alignment with its purpose and values. Think about how Yvon Chouinard masterfully led his people through difficult transitions, even when many of them initially resisted.

And think about how Teddy Raskin navigated the complexities of international aid to help so many people overcome unforeseen challenges.

You have the power within you to be just as effective at disrupting whatever you put your mind to. Go forth, *disrupt everything,* create meaningful relationships, and *live your good life.*

Part VII
Your Positive Disrupter Toolkit

About These Worksheets

Many of the questions and exercises that follow are geared for your use as an individual in your career and/or personal life. However, we've flagged some with the label "[FOR TEAMS]" when they specifically apply to your team, department, company, nonprofit, or other group. To fit your situation, think of the label "team" in the broadest possible sense.

Also, if you don't want to write in this book, or if you can't because you're reading the ebook edition or listening to the audiobook, you can download free printable PDFs of these nine tools. Just visit **jamespatterson.com/disrupt-downloads**.

Tool 1: Identify the Fire Inside You

Part 1: The Three Elements of the Fire Inside

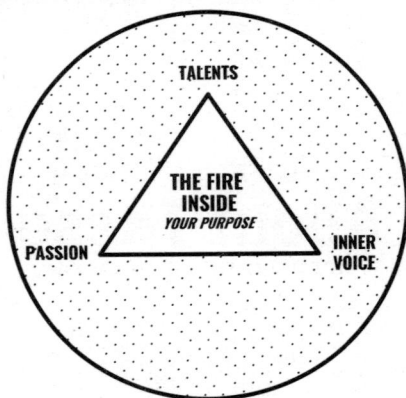

There is a fire inside you that exists at the intersection of your **Talent, Inner Voice,** and **Passion.** This worksheet will help you identify and connect these three elements.

Your Talents

Talent involves both what you're good at and what you're truly *great* at. Consider the unique abilities and skills that set you apart. Now is not the time for false modesty.

1. What activities or tasks do you excel at naturally?

....

....

....

....

....

....

2. What do people frequently ask for your help with?

....

....

....

....

....

3. What accomplishments are you most proud of?

....

....

....

....

4. [FOR TEAMS] What does your team do exceptionally well, relative to its peers?

....

....

....

....

5. [FOR TEAMS] If someone asks about your team's accomplishments, what comes to mind first?

....

....

....

....

....

Your Inner Voice

Your inner voice is informed by your experiences, knowledge, and beliefs. It steers you toward what inherently feels right because it meets a genuine need in the world.

1. What guides your decisions and actions?

....
....
....
....
....
....

2. When do you feel most at peace or fulfilled?

....
....
....
....
....
....

3. What experiences have shaped your perspective and drive?

....
....
....
....
....

4. [FOR TEAMS] When do you feel like your team is functioning at its highest possible level?

....
....
....
....
....
....
....

Your Passion

Passion is the spark that lights the fire inside, igniting your enthusiasm and commitment.

1. What activities or causes make you feel excited and energized?

....
....
....
....
....
....
....
....

2. What do you enjoy doing so much that you lose track of time?

....
....
....
....
....
....
....

3. What would you do even if you weren't paid for it?

....
....
....
....
....
....
....

4. [FOR TEAMS] When do you feel like your team is most passionate about their efforts?

....
....
....
....
....
....

Part 2: Your Values as the Foundation of Your Purpose

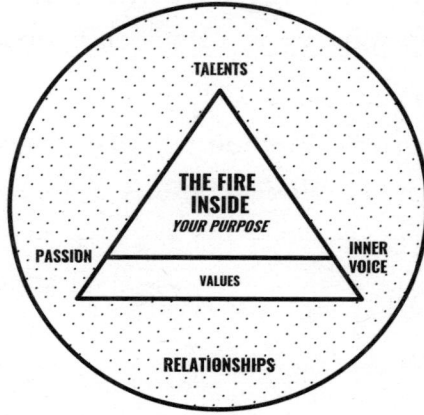

Values are fundamental beliefs and principles that guide your decisions. Below is a list of potential values to inspire you, as well as your family or team. These are simply provided to get you thinking and are not the only possible answers. Be creative when identifying your values.

Integrity	Duty	Loyalty
Honesty	Empathy	Trustworthiness
Compassion	Wisdom	Gratitude
Accountability	Humility	Inclusiveness
Courage	Kindness	Balance
Respect	Authenticity	Discipline
Innovation	Growth	Generosity
Perseverance	Fairness	Patience
Teamwork	Optimism	Determination
Excellence	Responsibility	
Faith	Creativity	

Identify three to five key values and define what each means to you and/or your team. Then ask yourself what actions illustrate the value in your everyday life or your team's collective efforts. Try to be specific.

1. Value: ....

What does this value mean to you?

....
....
....
....
....

What does this value look like in practice?

....
....
....
....
....

2. Value: ....

What does this value mean to you?

....
....
....
....
....

What does this value look like in practice?

....

....

....

....

3. Value: ....

What does this value mean to you?

....

....

....

....

What does this value look like in practice?

....

....

....

....

4. Value: ....

What does this value mean to you?

....

....

....

....

What does this value look like in practice?

....
....
....
....
....
....

5. Value: ....
What does this value mean to you?

....
....
....
....
....
....

What does this value look like in practice?

....
....
....
....
....
....
....

Tool 2: Craft Your Mission Statement

In the preface of this book, James Patterson stresses the importance of crafting a mission statement that captures the essence of what you're trying to accomplish. It's an essential step for both individuals and teams.

As a reminder, here is the blueprint he imagines for himself:

There's a story for everybody.
Don't get in the way of the story.
Tap into something in the psyche.
Get interested in the people in the middle.
Provide cathartic emotional experiences.

The questions you answered in Tool 1 will give you the raw material to craft your own mission statement.

Your Mission Statement—For Individuals

Refer back to your answers to the questions in Tool 1 to create a mission statement that reflects your talent, inner voice, and passion.

I will use my talent for

....
....
....
....
....
....
....

I will try to meet the needs of

....
....
....
....
....
....
....

In doing so, I will tap into my passion for

....
....
....
....
....
....
....
....

Examples

Musician

I will use my talent for songwriting and performing to meet the needs of audiences seeking connection and inspiration. In doing so, I will tap into my passion for evoking emotions and bringing people together through the power of music.

Firefighter

I will use my talent for quick decision-making and my capacity for physical endurance to meet the needs of communities in times of crisis. In doing so, I will tap into my passion for protecting lives and property, providing safety and reassurance to those in need.

Entrepreneur

I will use my talent for innovation and my business acumen to meet the needs of markets seeking novel solutions and growth. In doing so, I will tap into my passion for driving progress and creating dynamic ventures that transform industries and improve lives.

Your Mission Statement—For Teams

Combine your answers to the questions in Tool 1 to create a mission statement that reflects your team's talent, inner voice, and passion.

We will use our talent for ....

....

....

....

....

We will try to meet the needs of ....

....

....

....

....

In doing so, we will tap into our passion for ....

....

....

....

....

....

Examples

Start-up Engineering Team

We will use our talent for product development to build software that truly delights our B2B customers. In doing so, we will tap into our passion for exceeding expectations and making customers so excited that they willingly spread word of mouth about us.

Local Church's Food Bank Volunteers

We will use our talents for fundraising and community outreach to gather more food donations than ever this fall. We will help the growing ranks of neighbors who rely on our efforts to feed their families healthy meals. In doing so, we will tap into our passion for practicing our faith by loving our neighbors and giving people a helping hand while they get back on their feet.

Car Dealership's Sales Force

We will use our talent for empathy and our deep knowledge of cars to meet the needs of customers who trust us to provide reliable, comfortable, and appropriate vehicles. In doing so, we will tap into our passion for matching each customer with the car that best fits their needs and desires, knowing that the best way to maximize our income is by maximizing their satisfaction.

Tool 3: Tap into Your Experience

Take a step back. Look at your life. Recognize moments of being either the disrupter or the disrupted. Whether it's changing careers, moving to a new place, leading a new initiative, or navigating difficult conversations, each instance underscores your role as an agent of change. These experiences, big and small, showcase your adaptability, tenacity, and problem-solving skills.

Reflect: Past achievements can inspire you today. Documenting these successes and efforts helps reinforce your confidence in your own capabilities.

Repeat: Keep telling yourself: "I can handle this."

Remember: Previous strategies that have worked before may not always guarantee future success.

Recalibrate: Be open to adapting and finding new approaches when facing new challenges. But you can still find great value in recalling past challenges.

Reflecting on Your Personal Disruptions

Use the space on the next page to list some of the disruptions you've experienced in your career or personal life. Identify how you behaved, what you achieved, and what you learned from each.

Examples:

Disruption	How You Behaved	What You Achieved	What You Learned
Job loss	Networked, updated résumé, applied for new jobs	Found a better job	Resilience, value of networking

Disruption	How You Behaved	What You Achieved	What You Learned

Reflecting on Team Disruptions

If appropriate, now repeat the exercise with your team in mind. What significant challenges have you faced and over-come together?

Disruption	How You Behaved	What You Achieved	What You Learned

Tool 4: Inventory Your Resources

It's easy to feel like you don't have enough resources to launch a disruption. But in reality, you have a treasure trove of assets:

Knowledge, accessible through books, courses, and tutorials, can offer insights for any endeavor.

Technology, from the devices you use daily to advanced software, can revolutionize work.

Financial means, though they may seem sparse, can be maximized with smart planning.

Personal experience, enriched by consultations with mentors and colleagues, can uncover hidden assets and present untapped opportunities.

Sources of Support

List the resources you have available. Use the categories provided to spark your thinking. Each resource, from technology to personal expertise, acts as a tool to help you achieve your goals with creativity and resilience.

Category	Resource	Resource	Resource
People			
Time			
Energy			
Financing			
Knowledge			
Experience			
Technology			
Other Resources			

Resource Inventory Reflection

1. How can you effectively use the resources listed above?

....

....

....

....

2. What untapped opportunities or resources might you be overlooking?

....

....

....

....

....

....

3. Whom can you consult with to uncover additional resources you might not have initially recognized?

....

....

....

....

....

Use this inventory to remind yourself of the abundance of resources at your disposal. With thoughtful planning and strategic implementation, these resources can help you overcome challenges, achieve your goals, and disrupt everything!

Sources of Support for Teams

You can repeat the same exercise and reflection questions with your team, if appropriate. You probably have more resources at your disposal than you realize.

Category	Resource	Resource	Resource
People			
Time			
Energy			
Financing			
Knowledge			
Experience			
Technology			
Other Resources			

Resource Inventory Reflection for Teams

1. How can your team effectively use the resources listed on the previous page?

....
....
....
....
....
....

2. What untapped opportunities or resources might your team be overlooking?

....
....
....
....
....
....

3. Whom can your team consult with to uncover additional resources you might not have initially recognized?

....
....
....
....
....

Tool 5: Analyze Your Relationships

Relationships have the profound power to either ignite and nourish your inner fire or dampen and extinguish your zest and creativity. The connections you cultivate can lift you up and push you toward your dreams — or they can pull you down, anchoring you in place. Positive relationships act as tailwinds, pushing you toward your purpose and fueling the fire inside you. Negative relationships act as headwinds, holding you back and stifling your progress. Assessing both types of relationships and your role in them is crucial for personal growth.

Assessing Your Relationships

Use the table on the next page to list the key relationships in your life. These could be personal (family, friends, mentors) or professional (colleagues, leaders, team members).

Then rate each relationship on a scale from −5 to +5, based on its impact:

Headwinds (−5 to −1): These relationships create resistance, holding you back from your purpose.

Neutral (0): These relationships have little to no impact on your direction.

Tailwinds (+1 to +5): These relationships provide support and momentum, pushing you toward your purpose.

Relationship	Them to You											You to Them										
	Headwind Hold you back					Tailwind Push you forward						Headwind Hold them back					Tailwind Push them forward					
	−5	−4	−3	−2	−1	0	1	2	3	4	5	−5	−4	−3	−2	−1	0	1	2	3	4	5

Reflect on your strongest headwinds and tailwinds. Consider how you can reduce the drag of headwinds and maximize the lift from tailwinds.

By regularly assessing your relationships, you can ensure that you are surrounded by people who ignite and nourish your inner fire, helping you achieve your dreams and maintain your zest and creativity. Great relationships are mutually beneficial, so strive to be a tailwind for others as well.

Assessing Your Team's Relationships

For teams, relationships take the form of alliances with outside individuals and groups. Think of that church-run food bank that partners with local small businesses to put up flyers about their pre-Thanksgiving donation drive. Those are tailwind relationships for the team.

You can repeat the exercise on the previous page by thinking about the headwinds and tailwinds of the key individuals and groups your team frequently interacts with.

Rate each relationship on a scale from −5 to +5, based on its impact:

Headwinds (−5 to −1): These relationships create resistance, holding you back from your purpose.

Neutral (0): These relationships have little to no impact on your direction.

Tailwinds (+1 to +5): These relationships provide support and momentum, pushing you toward your purpose.

Relationship	Them to You												You to Them											
	Headwind Hold you back						Tailwind Push you forward						Headwind Hold them back						Tailwind Push them forward					
	−5	−4	−3	−2	−1	0	1	2	3	4	5	−5	−4	−3	−2	−1	0	1	2	3	4	5

Tool 6: Discern Your Ideal Role (for Now)

Facing a disruption and unsure where to begin, what steps to take, or what role to play? Use this worksheet to gain clarity and begin to map your path forward.

Describe a current situation, from your point of view, in which you are unsure of your next steps.

....

....

....

....

....

....

....

....

....

....

....

....

Now think more deeply about the situation you just wrote about. Reflect on the actions you are inclined to take and how they compare with the ideal actions that the situation might be calling for.

What do you feel inclined to do?

....

....

....

....

What is the situation asking or requiring you to do?

....

....

....

....

Using the chart below, put a star (★) where you feel inclined to act and a circle (O) where you believe the situation requires you to be.

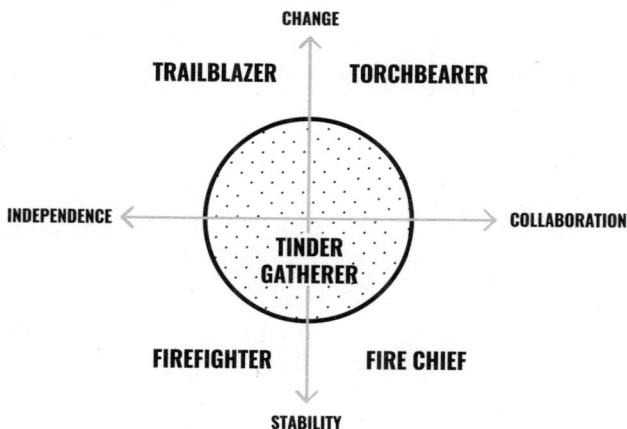

Is there a gap between what you feel inclined to do and what you believe the situation requires? If so, how would you describe the size of and reason for this gap?

Based on your assessment, which of the five disruptive roles (Trailblazer, Firefighter, Torchbearer, Fire Chief, Tinder Gatherer) do you believe you should take on, at least for now, to confront this situation?

....
....
....
....
....
....
....
....
....
....
....
....
....

Discerning an Ideal Role for Your Team

This assessment is also appropriate for teams, because teams often need to choose one of these five disruptive roles to make the most progress toward their overall mission. For instance, that church food bank team may see themselves as torchbearers, leading others in their community to get involved in confronting a local food crisis.

Describe a current situation in which your team is unsure of its next steps.

....
....
....
....
....
....
....
....
....

Now think more deeply about the situation you just wrote about. Reflect on the actions your team is inclined to take and how they compare with the ideal actions that the situation might be calling for.

What do you feel inclined to do?

....
....
....
....

What is the situation asking or requiring you to do?

....
....
....
....

Using the chart below, put a star (★) where you feel inclined to act and a circle (O) where you believe the situation requires you to be.

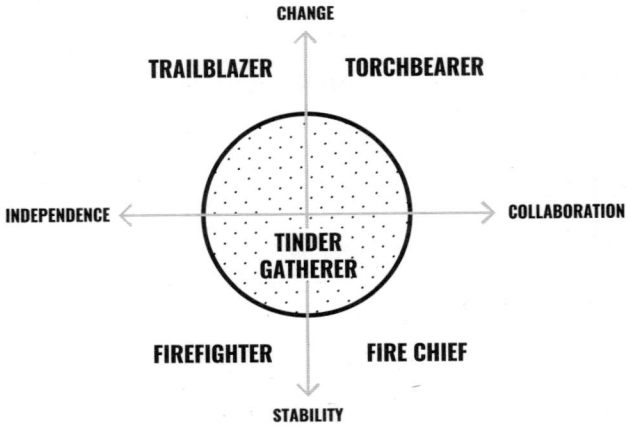

CHANGE

TRAILBLAZER   TORCHBEARER

INDEPENDENCE ← → COLLABORATION

TINDER GATHERER

FIREFIGHTER   FIRE CHIEF

STABILITY

Is there a gap between what you feel inclined to do and what you believe the situation requires? If so, how would you describe the size of and reason for this gap?

Based on your assessment, which of the five disruptive roles do you believe your team should take on, at least for now, to confront this situation?

....
....
....
....
....
....
....

Tool 7: Assess Your 16 Key Behaviors

Evaluate your actions in the following areas on a scale of 1 to 5, with 1 being the least often and 5 being the most often.

Body Part	Behavior	Score	Total Body Part Score
BRAIN	I think deeply in order to uncover insights		
	I exercise my brain muscles regularly		
EYES	I have a vision for the future		
	I look carefully at the present moment		
EARS	I listen closely in order to understand others		
	I hear what isn't being said		
MOUTH	I say something smart when communicating		
	I repeat key messages to ensure understanding		
HEART	I care for the needs of other people		
	I act based on my conscience		

(continues)

Body Part	Behavior	Score	Total Body Part Score
GUT	I trust my instincts (and they're worth trusting)		
	I persevere during uncomfortable times		

Body Part	Behavior	Score	Total Body Part Score
HANDS	I let go of good things in order to pursue great ones		
	I roll up my sleeves and get involved		

Body Part	Behavior	Score	Total Body Part Score
FEET	I run toward disruption		
	I stand steady during uncertain times		

Once you've scored your actions, add your total points for each body part. Consider which areas you're strong in and which might require focus and improvement.

Thinking About the 16 Key Behaviors for Teams

Like individuals, teams tend to be better at some of these behaviors than others, which makes them better suited for some types of disruption rather than others. It can be useful to think about how your team does in the same areas, using the same 1-to-5 scale.

Body Part	Behavior	Score	Total Body Part Score
BRAIN	We think deeply in order to uncover insights		
	We exercise our brain muscles regularly		
EYES	We have a vision for the future		
	We look carefully at the present moment		
EARS	We listen closely to understand each other		
	We hear what isn't being said		
MOUTH	We're good at communicating, internally and externally		
	We repeat key messages to ensure understanding		
HEART	We care for one another's needs		
	We act based on our collective principles		
GUT	We trust our instincts (and they're worth trusting)		
	We persevere during uncomfortable times		

(continues)

Body Part	Behavior	Score	Total Body Part Score
HANDS	We let go of good things in order to pursue great ones		
	We roll up our sleeves and share the dirty work		

FEET	We run toward disruption		
	We stand steady during uncertain times		

Once you've scored your team's actions, add the total points for each body part. Consider which areas your team is strong in and which might require focus and improvement.

Tool 8: Refine Your Positive Disrupter Loop

Refinement involves reviewing your results, interpreting what they mean, revising your expectations and approach, and committing to getting better. This process sets the Positive Disrupter Loop into motion again. Use this self-assessment tool to document what went well, note where there are opportunities to improve, and plan your next steps.

Step 1: Review Your Achievements

Describe a project you recently completed or results you recently delivered.

....

....

....

....

....

What were your specific goals or objectives?

....

....

....

....

....

....

What were the actual results?

....

....

....

....

....

....

....

Did you meet, exceed, or fall short of your expectations?

....

....

....

....

....

....

....

What were the key factors that contributed to your outcomes?

....

....

....

....

....

....

....

Step 2: Reflect on Your Achievements

What do these results reveal about your strengths?

....
....
....
....
....

What do these results reveal about your weaknesses?

....
....
....
....
....

What have you learned from this experience?

....
....
....
....
....

How do these results align with your values and long-term goals?

....
....
....
....

Step 3: Revise Your Plans or Approach

What changes can you make to your strategy to improve future results?

....
....
....
....

Are there any resources or support systems you need to seek out?

....
....
....
....

What new skills or knowledge do you need to acquire?

....
....
....
....

How can you adjust your expectations to be either more realistic or more ambitious?

....
....
....
....
....

Step 4: Recommit to Next Steps

What are your revised goals or objectives?

....
....
....
....
....

What specific actions will you take to achieve these goals?

....
....
....
....
....

How will you hold yourself accountable to these commitments?

....
....
....
....
....

What will success look like for you in this next phase?

....
....
....
....

Refinement for Teams

This refinement process is useful for teams as well as individuals. All of the questions on the previous pages can also be asked and answered about your team, to explore what's currently going well, where you're falling short, and what you might start doing differently.

Step 1: Review Your Team's Achievements

Write down a project your team recently completed or results you recently delivered.

....
....
....
....
....
....
....

What were your specific goals or objectives?

....
....
....
....
....
....
....

JAMES PATTERSON

What were the actual results?

....

....

....

....

....

....

....

....

Did you meet, exceed, or fall short of your expectations?

....

....

....

....

....

....

....

What were the key factors that contributed to your outcomes?

....

....

....

....

....

....

....

Step 2: Reflect on Your Achievements

What do these results reveal about your strengths?

....
....
....
....
....

What do these results reveal about your weaknesses?

....
....
....
....
....

What have you learned from this experience?

....
....
....
....
....

How do these results align with your values and long-term goals?

....
....
....
....

JAMES PATTERSON

Step 3: Revise Your Plans or Approach

What changes can you make to your strategy to improve future results?

....

....

....

....

....

Are there any resources or support systems you need to seek out?

....

....

....

....

What new skills or knowledge do you need to acquire?

....

....

....

....

How can you adjust your expectations to be either more realistic or more ambitious?

....

....

....

....

Step 4: Recommit to Next Steps

What are your revised goals or objectives?

....
....
....
....
....

What specific actions will you take to achieve these goals?

....
....
....
....
....

How will you hold yourself accountable to these commitments?

....
....
....
....
....

What will success look like for you in this next phase?

....
....
....
....

Closing Thoughts

Refinement is an ongoing process. By consistently reviewing, reflecting, revising, and recommitting, you and your team can set yourselves up for continual improvement and greater achievements. Use this worksheet regularly to keep the Positive Disrupter Loop in motion and to continue to throw fuel on your fire inside.

Tool 9: Chart Your Disruptive Path

Use this worksheet to explore how disruption can help you achieve your desired results. By following the key steps on the following pages, you will systematically analyze disruption, derive actionable insights, and develop a plan to bring your ideas to life.

The nine blocks on the worksheet spell out the word *disrupter.*

Disruption
Insights
Situation
Results
Use
Plan
Tell
Execute
Refine

The same questions that apply to you as an individual can also apply to your team. You may wish to download extra copies so you can repeat this exercise more than once, or as a group.

See **jamespatterson.com/disrupt-downloads**.

Disruption

Question: What is the disruption (e.g., change, incident, crisis, trend) under consideration?

Instructions: Begin by clearly defining the specific disruption you're addressing. Whether it's a sudden change, an ongoing trend, an unexpected incident, or a crisis, provide details that help explain its context and scope.

Insights

Question: How is the disruption reshaping opportunities and expectations?

Instructions: Consider how the disruption is changing the landscape of your environment, industry, or situation. Identify new opportunities that have emerged as a result of this disruption and consider how the expectations of stakeholders, customers, and team members might be shifting in response.

Situation

Question: How would you describe your current situation?

Instructions: Assess and describe your current position in relation to the disruption. Highlight the challenges you face as well as the strengths you possess that can help you navigate the situation effectively.

Results

Question: What are your current and desired results?

Instructions: Clearly state the outcomes you are experiencing. Then specify the results you aim to achieve in response to the disruption, making a clear distinction between your current status and your desired goals.

Use

Question: How can you apply the insights you identified above to achieve your desired results?

Instructions: Think about how the insights you've gathered can be applied to move you toward your desired results. Consider practical steps and actions that can leverage these insights effectively and outline how you plan to implement them.

Plan

Question: What is your plan to bring your idea to life (e.g., who, when, and how)?

Instructions: Create a detailed action plan that outlines the steps needed to achieve your desired results. Specify who will be responsible for each part of the plan. Establish a clear timeline for implementation, and explain how each step will be carried out.

Tell

Question: Whom do you need to tell or inform?

Instructions: Identify the people or groups who need to be informed about your plan and its progress. Determine the best ways to communicate with these stakeholders, whether through meetings, emails, or reports, ensuring that everyone is kept in the loop.

Execute

Question: How will you execute implementation?
Instructions: Describe how you will track the progress of your plan. Set up review mechanisms for assessing progress and make adjustments as needed. Assign oversight roles to individuals who will be responsible for various parts of the plan.

Refine

Question: How will you capture lessons learned?
Instructions: Establish methods for collecting feedback throughout the implementation process. Make a plan for noting what worked well and what didn't, and consider how you will use these lessons to improve future actions and plans.

Disrupter Worksheet: Chart Your Disruptive Path

D	DISRUPTION
What is the disruption (e.g., change, incident, crisis, trend)?	

I	INSIGHTS
How is the disruption reshaping opportunities and expectations?	

U	USE
How could you apply the insights to achieve desired results?	

T	TELL
Who do you need to tell or involve?	

S	SITUATION
How would you describe your current situation?	

R	RESULTS
What are your current and desired results?	

P	PLAN
What is your plan to bring your ideas to life (e.g., who, what, when, how)?	

E	EXECUTE
How will you execute implementation?	

R	REFINE
How will you capture lessons learned?	

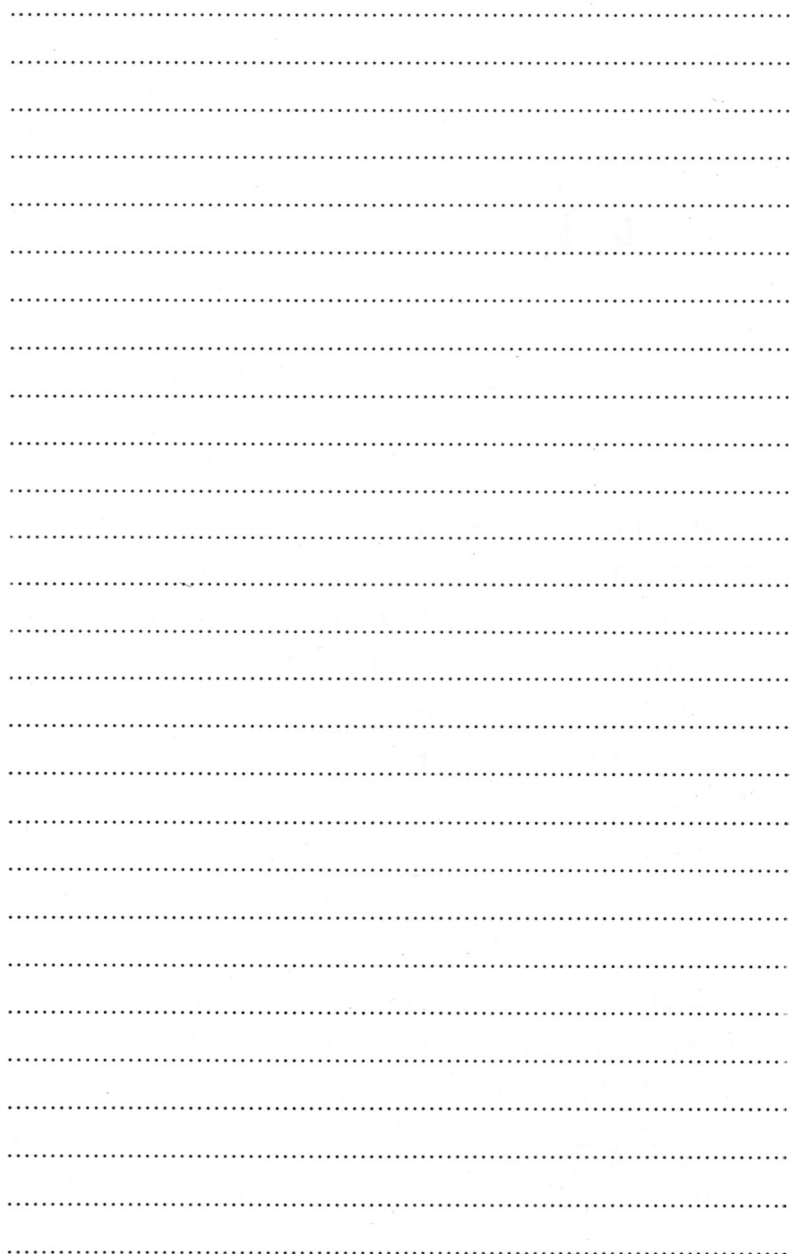

Acknowledgments

Researching and writing *Disrupt Everything* required gathering input, insights, and ideas from many people. First, we want to extend our deepest gratitude to the hundreds of individuals who generously sat for interviews and the thousands who participated in surveys. Your responses were instrumental in shaping the content of this book, and without your voices, this project would not have been possible. Your experiences and insights have truly brought this book to life.

We want to acknowledge our incredible research-team members: Taylor Ward, Kacie Ryan, Ella Nordlie, Ethan Herr, Erin O'Connor, Griffin Murch, Stefania Yee, and Lydia Liu. Your dedication to this project has been invaluable.

Patrick thanks his wife and partner in every

adventure, Jamie, along with their children and grand-children: Alex, Kevin, Clementine, Marigold, Clay, and Jess. Their love, laughter, and support make the journey worthwhile.

Bibliography

The stories that open each chapter in this book are based largely on an original interview with the person featured in the story. The authors consulted other accounts of these persons in the articles listed here.

Part I: Fire, Fuel, and Four Facts

Chapter 1: The Fire Inside You

Piphus, Megan. Original interview, September 14, 2022.

Harris-Perry, Melissa, host. *The Takeaway,* podcast. "Bringing Black Girl Magic to the Voice of Sesame Street's Gabrielle." WYNCStudios, September 29, 2022. https://www.wnycstudios .org/podcasts/takeaway/segments/bringing-black-girl-magic -voice-sesame-streets-gabrielle.

Kaur, Harmeet. "She Grew up Watching Sesame Street. Then She Made History as the Show's First Female Puppeteer." CNN, February 26, 2023. https://www.cnn.com/2023/02/26/enter tainment/sesame-street-megan-piphus-peace-cec/index.html.

Cilik, Anton (@antoncilik7080). "Megan Piphus Ventriloquism Act Americas Got Talent s08 Audition." YouTube, June 13, 2013.

BIBLIOGRAPHY

Video, 4 min., 17 sec. https://www.youtube.com/watch?v
=JrJqoU6ipcs.

Altvater, Desjah. "A Peek Inside Her Agenda: Megan Piphus Peace."
HerAgenda, February 20, 2023. https://heragenda.com/p/megan
-piphus-peace/.

Piphus, Megan (@meganpiphus). Instagram. https://www.insta
gram.com/meganpiphus/reel/C0hnAL1ux8W/.

Chapter 2: The Fuel for the Fire Inside

Farrand, Bevin. Original interview, September 20, 2023.

Farrand, Bevin. "I Made $297,000 in 18 Months as a Personal-
Brand Consultant. Here's How I Found Clients and Built My
One-Woman Business After Being Laid Off." *Business Insider,*
September 26, 2022. https://www.businessinsider.com/laid-off
-started-coaching-business-made-six-figures-2022-9.

Chapter 3: Fact 1: The Status Quo Is a Deceptive Little Devil

Andrew, Jamie. Original interview, October 19, 2019.

"What You Did Next: Jamie Andrew." *Edit: The University of Edinburgh Alumni Magazine,* Winter 2014. https://alumni.ed.ac.uk/sites
/default/files/atoms/files/edit-winter2014-_spreads.pdf.

Chapter 4: Fact 2: You're Wired to Disrupt

Wayans, Marlon. Original interview, August 7, 2023.

Biography.com Editors. "Marlon Wayans." Biography, December
4, 2019. https://www.biography.com/actors/marlon-wayans.

Marchese, David. "Marlon Wayans on 'Good Grief' and the Death
of His Parents." *New York Times,* May 4, 2024. https://www
.nytimes.com/2024/05/04/magazine/marlon-wayans-inter
view.html.

Wayans, Marlon (@marlonwayans). Instagram. https://www
.instagram.com/marlonwayans/p/BsgThu1H00i/.

Chapter 5: Fact 3: Relationships Provide Headwinds and Tailwinds

Frierson, Trina. Original interview, March 6, 2024.

Park, Jeremy C. "Mending Hearts Efforts to Help Women Overcome Addiction." *City Current* (Nashville Radio Show), November 26, 2022. https://citycurrent.com/2022/11/26/mending-hearts -efforts-to-help-women-overcome-addiction/.

Chapter 6: Fact 4: Your Time Here Is Finite—Make It Count in Ways That Matter

D'Eri, Tom. Original interview, December 14, 2023.

"Community Ally: Andrew and Tom D." AutismSpeaks, n.d. Video, 9 min., 43 sec. https://www.autismspeaks.org/profile /video-meet-andrew-and-tom-d.

Mendler, Adam. "Context Drives Behavior: Interview with Tom D'Eri, Co-Founder of Rising Tide Car Wash." AdamMendler. https://www.adammendler.com/blog/tom-deri.

Part II: The Positive Disrupter Loop

Chapter 7: Disruption on the Streets of India

Lindell Qwist, Pia. Original interviews, September 12, 2023, and April 30, 2024.

Ruglykke, Kristine Emery. "Kristine on Her Role as an Ambassador," Gadensboern.org. https://www.gadensboern.org/kristine -emery-ruglykke-1

Part III: Discern

Chapter 9: The Power of Discernment

Henderson, Mindy. Original interview, February 1, 2023.

PYMNTS Retail. "Dick's Sporting Goods: Shoppers Demand More Experiential Stores." PYMNTS, May 29, 2024. https:// www.pymnts.com/news/retail/2024/dicks-sporting-goods -shoppers-demand-more-experiential-stores/.

BIBLIOGRAPHY

Chapter 10: Trailblazer: Seek Change and Act Independently

Natori, Josie. Original interview, July 17, 2023.

Newswire. "Josie Natori Inducted into Accessories Council Hall of Fame." Press release, August 10, 2022. https://www.newswire .com/news/josie-natori-inducted-into-accessories-council-hall -of-fame-21791327.

Chapter 11: Firefighter: Seek Stability and Act Independently

Rodrigues, Harsha. Original interview, July 28, 2023.

Chapter 12: Torchbearer: Seek Change and Act Collaboratively

Milliken, Bill. Original interview, May 25, 2023.

Chapter 13: Fire Chief: Seek Stability and Act Collaboratively

Getty, Keith. Original interview, September 27, 2023.

"Hitting the Right Notes: Hymn Writer Keith Getty on Why It Took Him Some Time to Woo Wife Kristyn." *Belfast Telegraph,* August 11, 2018. https://www.belfasttelegraph.co.uk/life/week end/hitting-the-right-notes-hymn-writer-keith-getty-on -why-it-took-him-some-time-to-woo-wife-kristyn/37196805 .html.

"Hymn Writer Keith Getty Marks First Individual to Receive OBE Award Involved in World of Contemporary Church Music." Gospel Music Association, July 17, 2018. https://gospelmusic .org/news/hymn-writer-keith-getty-marks-first-individual -to-receive-obe-award-involved-in-world-of-contemporary -church-music.

Kramer McGinnis, Kelsey. "The Gettys' Modern Hymn Movement Has Theological Pull." *Christianity Today,* October 2, 2024. https://www.christianitytoday.com/2024/10/keith-kristyn -getty-sing-conference-nashville-modern-hymns-theology -worship/.

BIBLIOGRAPHY

Chapter 14: Tinder Gatherer: Pursue Clarity and Provide Support

Barnett, Robert. Original interview, May 2, 2023.

Part IV: Behave

Chapter 15: The Anatomy of a Positive Disrupter

Swanson, Dansby. Original interview, June 24, 2020.

Andracki, Tony. "'We Don't Do Losing': How Dansby Swanson Plans to Help the Cubs Return to Winning Ways." Marquee Sports Network, 2023. https://www.marqueesportsnetwork .com/we-dont-do-losing-how-dansby-swanson-plans-to-help -the-cubs-return-to-winning-ways/.

Chapter 16: Brain

Mendelson, David. Original interview, November 11, 2023.

"David Mendelson: Crain's 2022 Notable Leaders in Sustainabil- ity." Crain's Chicago Business, June 24, 2022. https://www.chi cagobusiness.com/awards/david-mendelson.

Chapter 17: Eyes

Anderson, Joel. Original interview, September 11, 2023.

Chapter 18: Ears

Ogle, Vanessa. Original interview, October 11, 2023.

Hall, Cheryl. "Vanessa Ogle Went into Creative Overdrive When Pandemic Threatened Her Plano Tech Company." *Dallas Morning News,* June 7, 2020. https://www.dallasnews.com/business /2020/06/07/vanessa-ogle-put-on-her-beanie-propeller-as-pan demic-threatened-her-hotel-tech-company/.

Chapter 19: Mouth

Lupica, Mike. Original interview, July 19, 2023.

BIBLIOGRAPHY

Chapter 20: Heart

Wallace, Alicia. Original interview, June 8, 2023.

Loyd, Tony, host. *Social Entrepreneur,* podcast. "Weaving Artisans and Markets Together with Alicia Wallace All Across Africa." Tony-Loyd, July 15, 2018. https://tonyloyd.com/weaving-artisans-and-markets-together-with-alicia-wallace-all-across-africa/.

Tossan, Caroline. "All Across Africa, Weaving a Better World." *Maison & Objet,* February 27, 2020. https://www.maison-objet.com/en/paris/magazine/the-story-behind/all-across-africa-weaving-a-better-world.

Chapter 21: Gut

McIntosh, Chris "Mac." Original interview, May 30, 2023.

Chapter 22: Hands

Whitney, Chris. Original interview, September 29, 2023.

Chapter 23: Feet

Campbell, Jeff. Original interview, May 15, 2023.

Part V: Achieve

Chapter 24: Disruptive Impact

Linkner, Josh. Original interview, July 5, 2023.

Chapter 25: Disrupt Your Relationships

Westlake, Lucy. Original interview, August 31, 2023.

Chapter 27: Disrupt Your Team

Calipari, John. Original interview, September 15, 2023.

Chapter 28: Disrupt Your Organization

Lawton, Hal. Original interview, November 2, 2023.
Ingram, John. Original interview, April 27, 2022.

Chapter 29: Disrupt Your Industry

Katz-Mayfield, Andy. Original interview, June 29, 2023.
Raider, Jeff. Original interview, September 14, 2023.

Part VI: Refine

Chapter 30: It Takes a Posse

Bial, Debbie. Original interview, July 13, 2023.
Ainslie, Michael. Original interview, July 15, 2023.
Collado, Shirley. Original interview, June 29, 2023.
Nelson-Nwachuku, Monique. Original interview, July 13, 2023.
Christiansen, Doug. Posse Annual Report, 2023, p. 9. https://www.possefoundation.org/uploads/reports/AR_23_38.pdf
Rajlin, Juan. Posse Annual Report, 2023, p. 53. https://www.possefoundation.org/uploads/reports/AR_23_38.pdf
Petraeus, David. Original interview, January 18, 2023.

Chapter 31: Overcoming Resistance to Disruption

Beavers, Jim. Original interview, July 21, 2020.

Chapter 32: Leading Through Disruption

Stanley, Vincent. Original interview, February 26, 2020.
Hung, MaiLee. "Bring Back Clean Climbing." Patagonia, February 4, 2022. https://www.patagonia.com/stories/bring-back-clean-climbing/story-116308.html.
Hawkins, Nick. "Patagonia's Director of Philosophy Wants Your Business to Be Responsible, Not Sustainable." Inc., September 18, 2023. https://www.inc.com/nick-hawkins/patagonias-director

-of-philosophy-wants-your-business-to-be-responsible-not
-sustainable.html.

Archie, Ayana. "The Founder of Patagonia Is Giving His Company
Away to Help Fight Climate Change." NPR, September 15,
2022. https://www.npr.org/2022/09/15/1123104499/patagonia
-founder-climate-change.

Chapter 33: Go Disrupt Something

Raskin, Teddy. Original interview, April 13, 2023.

Bain, Katie. "How an Annual Vanderbilt Dance Show Has Raised
Major Money for Good Causes in Nashville." *Billboard*, September
26, 2024. https://www.billboard.com/pro/lights-on-the-lawn
-dance-show-nashville-charity-mary-parrish-center-gryffin/.

About the Authors

James Patterson is one of the best-known and biggest-selling writers of all time. Among his creations are some of the world's most popular series, including Alex Cross, the Women's Murder Club, Michael Bennett and the Private novels. He has written many other number one bestsellers including collaborations with President Bill Clinton, Dolly Parton and Michael Crichton, stand-alone thrillers and non-fiction. James has donated millions in grants to independent bookshops and has been the most borrowed adult author in UK libraries for the past fourteen years in a row. He lives in Florida with his family.

Patrick Leddin, PhD, has extensive hands-on leadership experience: in the 82nd Airborne Division as an airborne ranger infantry officer and in the private sector as a senior business consultant at KPMG Consulting and FranklinCovey. He founded and built two successful companies and is a sought-after global speaker, a top-ranked podcast host, and the author of the *Wall Street Journal* bestseller *The 5-Week Leadership Challenge: 35 Action Steps to Become the Leader You Were Meant to Be.* While on the faculty at Vanderbilt University, he served as director of the practice of business studies and led the Disruption Project, a multiyear study of success in the face of disruption. *Disrupt Everything—and Win: Take Control of Your Future* is the first book he's coauthored with James Patterson.